# Henry James

BY GEORGES MARKOW-TOTEVY

*Translated by John Cumming*

*With a preface by Andre Maurois*

MINERVA PRESS

First American edition published in 1969
by arrangement with the Merlin Press, Ltd.

Library of Congress Catalog Card Number: 68-22175

Funk & Wagnalls, *A Division of* Reader's Digest Books, Inc.

Printed in the United States of America

CONTENTS

HENRY JAMES was a great writer who spent his whole life wandering in a literary limbo between the paradise of European culture and the hell that was the Golden Age of America. He was too sensitive to suffer the vulgarity of an environment inimical (as he thought) to the artist; he was also too much of a Bostonian puritan to feel completely at ease in the atmosphere of European realism. For the major part of his life he was uprooted. He admired French novelists, but found them too concerned with the sordid. He found some measure of spiritual comfort with the English aristocracy. The big houses set in extensive grounds, the beautiful young Englishwomen and the writers whom they entertained every weekend played the same part in his life as the Court in the lives of the moralists and poets of seventeenth century France. Like those writers of an earlier age, Henry James came to believe that a leisured society, heir to a civilization that had lasted for many years, was the environment in which the feelings might most effectively be nurtured.

In fact there was something naïvely romantic about this vision of an almost superhuman world preserved in the apartments of the Faubourg St-Germain or the houses of Mayfair. This worship of a gracious though seriously defective society can be explained only by the inferiority complex aroused in James by a social order to which he was a stranger. James believed that an extremely subtle art was necessary to express correspondingly fine shades of feeling. He delighted in the minute analysis of Europeans uprooted from their particular environments and living in American society; of American expatriates like himself; and of English people in their own country. Occasionally, he would condemn the decadence of Europe and describe its dangerous influence on a New England artist; sometimes he took as his theme an American who had crossed the Atlantic to save a young fellow countryman from a Frenchwoman, but who was seduced by the charm and candour of European womanhood.

The analytical style he created emphasized the importance of the incidental; in some respects, it was a style that foreshadowed that of Proust. James, like Proust, inhabited a universe of minute facts which attained to beauty when revealed and magnified by his method of projection. He found his best subjects in problems of artistic technique and in fantastic tales: many of his short stories concerned with these themes are masterpieces. The external world—the world of action—he rejected. Unlike the works of Balzac or of Proust, his novels were never based upon a concrete society. All his life full of vague longings and regrets, he remained at the entrance to countries of which he would have liked to become a citizen. In 1915 he made the symbolic gesture of adopting British nationality: this was certainly a form of emotional peace for James, although his spirit could not be naturalized.

Charles du Bos once said of James, whom he admired, 'He proceeds as if he had previously cleaned out some beautiful and spacious rooms for the sake of each of his superb themes, ensuring that not one speck of dust remains. His novels and short stories develop like chamber music, secure from any interruption.' This music of the intellect, with its constant, even tone, can prove irritating to some readers, whereas others find it fascinating. I am among the latter.

I have enjoyed reading Georges Markow-Totevy's book. He admires the works of Henry James as they should be admired: he illuminates the central themes. His exposition will help the reader to a deeper understanding of James' writings.

André Maurois

# *1. A Short Biography*

Born in New York in 1843, Henry James was six months old when his parents took him across the Atlantic to spend two years in England and in France: his first childhood memory was related to the Place Vendôme. Can this not be taken as a sign of predestination for the future international novelist?

His father, Henry James Senior—of Irish descent, and the son of a very prosperous Albany, N.Y. merchant—had abandoned the family Calvinism while a young man and had set out to discover a superior faith, only to find his gods (Swedenborg and Fourier) in Europe. He devoted his life to the gospel of Swedenborgian cosmology and utopian socialism, propagating in America his newly found faith by means of lectures and theological and philosophical books—which won only a very meagre public. Impulsive and eccentric, he earned the judgement that he had 'the look of a broker, and the brains and heart of a Pascal'. His ideas, 'father's *ideas*'—as his son ironically called them—were, despite his somewhat naïve liberalism and optimism, not entirely valueless as a system of ethics. He protested against the religious 'sentimentality' of his time and sought after 'religion in the old virile sense', convinced that 'we are creatures with a lack, a destitution, a dearth, an ultimate helplessness', and that 'life is no farce; that it is not genteel comedy even; that it flowers and fructifies out of the profoundest tragic depths'.

Above all he condemned what he called the 'flagrant morality' of society and advocated a conscious moral sense; the betterment of mankind was his main concern. His ideas were the expression of a search not for happiness but for in-

1

tegrity and nobility of soul : to transform evil into good, to be capable of endurance and of sacrifice, to know how to discover greatness even in degradation. . . . He believed that man should forge for himself a superior social conscience, after being internally 'refined out of that supreme love of self and the world that alone constitutes hell'. A man of great culture, Henry James Senior possessed a deep love for life. Far removed from the literal and the obvious, his mind dealt with the appraisement of perceptions and relations, with those values that might completely satisfy spirit and taste. His son Henry was strongly affected by his convictions, although he later rejected religious and social optimism.

The novelist had a sister, Alice, and three brothers : Wilkinson was to die young, Robertson lived for many years in the West, but the eldest, William—later to become the well-known psychologist and pragmatist philosopher—would remain the closest associate of Henry James' life and career. Together, parents and sons formed an unusual household; the constant discussions, the exchange of ideas and impressions transformed everyday life into an unparalleled adventure. The prestige of European culture was supreme among them: the father knew Carlyle and Thackeray personally; eventually they all read— through the years—Dickens and Balzac, George Eliot and George Sand, *Punch* and *La Revue des Deux Mondes*. The family had many friends—artists, writers and travellers—who often came to the house. James Senior was on friendly terms with Thoreau, Hawthorne and Emerson, and he participated in the New England cultural revival. But these contacts with America were based only on intellectual grounds, and although the Jameses displayed an eager curiosity for the reality and environment around them, they remained detached from the practical and materialistic pursuits of their fellow-citizens. Instead, in their 'collective disconnectedness', they lived in a mythical world of their own fashion, poised, as it were, in mid air between New York and London, Boston and Paris.

After a childhood passed in Albany and in New York, Henry James travelled with his family in Europe from 1855 to 1860.

Somewhat desultorily, with an equal degree of irregularity, he studied at private institutions in Geneva, Bonn, Paris and Boulogne. This was no less *exposure* and *education* in Jamesian terms, and while still in his teens he became acquainted with the languages and cultures of Europe, which developed within him a diversity of outlandish and colourful impressions. At this time he was already an inveterate scribbler, writing prose narratives and plays or translating fables of La Fontaine, and pages from Schiller's *Maria Stuart*.

James Senior organized his sons' education according to his original ideals. It followed Rousseau's naturalistic philosophy, for it was conceived under no other rigour than the law of independent happen-as-it-may development, away from the restrictions imposed by a determined religion, social class or country. He allowed his children free contact with the world, but he never failed to impress upon them the necessity for constant spiritual tension to 'convert' any trial into moral training. Any encounter and impression became a lesson for greater sensitivity and curiosity in life, '. . . The authors and guardians of our youth', Henry James wrote, 'had virtually said to us but one thing, directed our course but by one word, though constantly repeated : Convert, convert, convert. . . . We were to convert and convert . . . simply everything that should happen to us . . . everything, every contact, every impression and every experience we should know. . . .' Thus James learned, early to analyse reality, to reduce external happenings to perception and feeling, to look always at 'the other side of the medal'.

Imagination and the absence of discipline characterized his up-bringing in all its phases. His formal schooling revealed, unruffled disdain for continuity and method : he went from French governesses to Scottish tutors, from American grade-schools to transatlantic pensions, with the same remarkable ease. One could almost say that he was essentially self-taught; all that he learned came from his precocious observation and abundant reading. 'The literal played in our education he has stated, as small a part as it perhaps ever played in any, and we wholesomely breathed inconsistency and ate and drank contradictions. The presence of paradox . . . was bright among us. . . .'

From childhood James was accustomed to face foreign and adverse conditions, to live at home in a more or less odd environment. His father was a most unusual man : a visionary philosopher, an invalid (who lost a leg in early life), a cosmopolitan without a real profession and living upon investments : certainly unlike the fathers of young Henry's schoolmates. Still less did his family resemble other American families : Henry soon had to realize that it did not belong to a particular social class, church or category of everyday life; too many 'impulsive journeyings', 'aimless vacillations' on both sides of the Atlantic, had finally endowed the family group with a distinct character that could not easily be placed : 'We all formed together quite a monstrous exception. . . .' James would say years later. His conviction was strong that he and his brothers were not like 'other' children; they were set *aside*, and this made him constantly eager to 'exchange my lot for that of somebody else, on the assured certainty of gaining by the bargain' . . . 'to *be* other, other almost anyhow, seemed as good as the probable taste of the bright compound wistfully watched at the confectioner's window'.

To this was added solitude, for Henry James grew up almost without friends. 'All boys, I rather found, were difficult to play with—unless it was that they rather found *me* !' Within the family, relations between brothers and between sons and parents were not relaxed : a general nervous strain and a tacit though continual rivalry existed with the genuine cordial amenity. Rather shy and uncommunicative by nature, James could not force himself to vie in humour and eloquence. His friend Perry remarked that Henry James' spirits were never so high as those of the others. If they had been, he still would have had but little chance in a conflict of will with them, on account of his slow speech, his halting choice of words'. He resisted the family exuberance by transforming his secret inferiority into a sort of 'fatalism of patience', if not resentment. The result was a lack of self-confidence : he became a dreamy and reticent child, a 'devourer of libraries, and an immense writer of novels and dramas'.

The reaction to being different, not less than his irregular education and travels, separated James from his contemporaries, his family and his country. From now on a sense of rootlessness, a sense of his own *aloneness* would dominate him.

He suffered especially from the traits and conditions that seemed to contract him for ever to William, his elder by only a year and four months. 'The only difference there is between Willy's and Harry's labours', Wilky notes on the subject of the youthful literary work of his brothers, 'is that the former always shows his productions while the modest little Henry wouldn't let a soul or even a spirit see his.' William, lively and aggressive by nature, appeared always to the fore in any new activity, expressed himself with ease, and made friends quickly. Henry envied him these qualities and was ambitious to equal him, but William 'was always round the corner and out of sight'. Tormented by his fruitless efforts to compete, he thought himself condemned to 'an inexhaustible brotherhood', and he never succeeded in taking the lead. He thought himself naturally relegated to the position of observer in the family circle; he found consolation only with his mother, whose resigned mildness and acceptance he shared.

When he returned to America after his stay in Europe from 1855 to 1860, James passed a restless youth in Newport, Boston and Cambridge. During these uncertain years, he tried painting as a career in the studio of William Hunt, and law at Harvard. He seemed always to be waiting, impatiently setting his dreams and unsatisfied desires in the future : 'never was an ingenuous youth more passionately and yet more patiently eager for what life might bring'. This indecision and somehow melancholic expectation were partly due to his unstable childhood, but in particular, the indirect, moral consequences of his 'horrid even if an obscure hurt', sustained while, at age eighteen, he helped to put out a fire at Newport. Exact details of the nature of this spinal strain are not available : James himself referred to it only seldom and in the vaguest of terms—an ambiguous attitude which has given rise to many suspicions, some even discerning here the reason for a latent invalidism or possibly sexual impotence. Although he complained later, at different occasions, of severe pains in the back, the effects were not serious, for he lived an active and hard-working life. If one can venture to call James an invalid, it is only in a mental and not a physical sense. He would seem to have seized upon this accident with eagerness to justify his psychological peculiarities, his estrangement from the world and experience. Reminded possibly of his father's invalid condition, his injury suddenly appeared to him as an event of cardinal importance, 'the effects of which were to draw themselves out incalculably and intolerably'. '. . . The twenty minutes [of the accident] had sufficed . . . at all events, to establish a relation—a relation to everything occurring round me, not only for the next four years but for long afterward—that was at once extraordinarily intimate and quite awkwardly irrelevant.' One critic has suggested that the tone of this passage is characteristic of a self-inflicted psychic wound, intellectualizing his fear of personal inadequacy as inevitable and final, and equating them with fatality. From that point on James accepted *his* 'otherness', his solitary destiny as a man denied of all commitment to living. This physical test determined his introverted attitude by supplying him with a valid motivation and, almost, an excuse.

His accident occurred during the Civil War, when his brothers Wilkinson and Robertson, and all the young men of his age, were fighting : he remained a stranger to the enthusiasm which possessed his generation, a mere witness to this historical crisis of his country. During the next ten years, he was often ill and did not indulge in the normal activities and pleasures proper to his youth. Then he fell in love with his cousin Minny Temple—'the very heroine of our common scene', as he used to refer to her—a lively girl impatient to know life and Europe, but consumptive and doomed. Was he really in love or did he just admire her? Here again, exact details are lacking and the nature of the relationship is difficult to determine. Two other admirers of Minny, also friends of James, had returned recently from the war, enveloped in an aura of bravery and manly vigour; extremely reserved, if not timid, and often sick, James assumed his usual attitude in this lovers' rivalry—that of a resigned observer. He was already convinced of the impossibility of effusive feelings and the denial of personal happiness. But there was also some regret in this, and he hoped for the day when he would be 'more active and masculine' in this friendship. Later, after Minny's death, he was to write : 'It comes home to me with irresistible power, the sense of how much I knew her and how much I loved her'. As with his other trials, this one could only be completely experienced when sublimated : 'converted' by the power of imagination, Minny was to emerge as the principal and most idealized heroine of his works : 'her image will preside in my intellect and twenty years hence what a pure eloquent vision she will be !'

The family wealth spared James the immediate necessity of choosing a career or of earning a living; this set him free to cultivate his literary vocation. From 1864, his first critical reviews began to appear in the *North American Review* and the *Nation*, soon to be followed by a few short stories and novels. Little by little he was winning a modest place in the world of American letters, but this precarious success did not cancel his mental restlessness. Wishing to recover health and moral equilibrium, he spent the years 1869-70 and 1872-74 in England, France and Italy, travelling and writing. The experiment proved to be beneficial on all accounts, and so, in 1875, he decided to establish himself permanently in Europe.

The Old World had played a major part in his up-bringing : '. . . the nostalgic cup,' he said, '. . . had been applied to my lips even before I was conscious of it. I was ever afterwards to feel that poison has entered my veins.' He and his brothers had grown up as 'hotel children'—gaping and wondering at Europe during their long peregrinations abroad; this had been the beginning of a lasting intellectual uprooting, as well as of a gradual separation from American life. In Europe, young

Henry had caught glimpses of what 'style' and 'glory', beauty
and history, could intensely embody and project—'the world,
in fine, raised to the richest and noblest expression'. When he
reached maturity he experienced the same veneration (and he
sensed again his inferiority) toward the age-old civilisation of
Europe : he considered it a 'complex fate being an American',
for the cultured American was bound to live isolated, lost in
the intellectual vacuum of his immense country, while his spirit
wandered in 'perpetual exile'. The United States of the 1860s,
with its utilitarian and industrial prosperity, had little to offer a
young man like James, whose sensitivity and taste were of the
'finer kind'.

Therefore, it is not surprising that the choice between
Europe and America became a pressing matter. He thought of
himself as a 'passionate pilgrim' to Europe whose road lay beyond the immediate limits of his fervour : to be an expatriate
meant facing an unknowable future of sensations and dis-
coveries far greater than what he could hope for in America.
'My choice is the old world,' he confessed himself in his *Notebooks*, 'my choice, my need, my life. . . . My work lies there—
and with this vast new world *je n'ai que faire*[1] . . . I could
remember without effort with what an irresistible longing I
turned to Europe, with what ardent yet timid hopes, with what
indefinite yet inspiring intentions, I took leave of *les miens*'.[1]

Chauvinistic criticism has reproached James for this decision
to leave his native country, forgetting however that he had
almost no other alternative : for intimate reasons which
detached him from America, his generation and even his
family, he could only be himself when away from them, safe to
establish at a distance a new relation of close ties and feelings
for them. His exile offered him escape, but also made less
obvious his 'otherness'; it became a justification for it. To live
in Europe meant searching for interior stability and finding an
intellectual climate more favourable to his artistic creation :
only there was he free to unleash his talents and his personality.

In 1875 (James was thirty-two), he first settled in Paris, 'the

[1] In French in the original text.

city of [his] dreams' : he was perfectly acquainted with the French language and customs. He became friendly with the great expatriate Russian novelist Turgenev and regularly attended Flaubert's 'Sundays', where he met the writers of the naturalistic group, destined to dominate the literary scene of the next two decades: Zola, Edmond de Goncourt, Taine, Daudet and Maupassant. In such company, however, little attention was paid to the reserved young foreigner whom no one knew. James soon achieved a 'satiety with the French mind', grew tired of the superficiality and brilliancy of 'la vie mondaine', and summarized his stay thus : 'A good deal of Boulevard and third-rate Americanism . . . I know the Théâtre français by heart.' He despaired of ever becoming a true Parisian and left the city in 1876, rather disappointed.

He established himself in London, where he spent his last forty years. Suddenly 'turning English all over', he readily submitted to what he called the 'Londonizing process', trying 'to feed only on English life, and the contact of English minds'. There was a natural bond of language and thought, of morality and wit, between the English and himself; he particularly admired the Victorian decorum of propriety and refinement, the meticulous control of feelings and gestures that extended beyond the discursive brilliancy, the light, temperamental attitudes of the French. He was soon drawn into the whirl of social life—whether by preference and enjoyment, or by his curiosity as a novelist. English customs and manners were ultimately more accessible and closer to him than those of America, because he saw them not as pre-ordained conditions but as new phenomena to be studied and mastered : '. . . London is on the whole the most possible form of life : I take it as an artist and as a bachelor; as one who has the passion of observation and whose business is the study of human life. It is the biggest aggregation of human life—the most complete compendium of the world . . . I felt all this in the autumn of 1876, when I first took up my abode in Bolton Street.'

After only a few years he thought of himself as English in everything except name, and his enthusiasm for England would

remain. Toward the end of the century, he tried continually
to render 'England in fiction—as the place I see most today
and, in a sort of way, know best'. He relied on America 'for
effect, no longer', although he again had recourse to it for the
subject-matter of his last works. He never detached himself
completely from his homeland, and, until the end of his life,
maintained the many friendships and memories which related
him to it; he went back for long visits at three different times,
in 1881-82, in 1904 and in 1910. After his parents' deaths
(1882) and that of his brother Wilky (1883), he remained in
closer contact with his brother William, in whom he now
readily confided and whose advice and criticism he readily
accepted. He grew increasingly attached to William's family,
to his nephew Henry above all, who came to take long holidays
with him in England. His sister Alice, after she suffered from
a nervous disorder and became almost an invalid, spent her last
ten years in England, and died there in 1892. The direct bonds
gradually loosened, but James continued to correspond with
several American friends whom he also met on different occasions on the Continent: J. R. Lowell, C. E. Norton, Grace
Norton, W. D. Howells, Henry Adams and, later, Edith
Wharton. After his trip of 1904, he paid a final tribute to his
native country in the essay *The American Scene*.

His life in England was almost completely devoid of incident;
he played no part in public life, never allowed himself to be
involved in a political or intellectual controversy, never joined
any literary clique, and cannot really be said to have had any
private life. He is one bachelor who has left no record of a love
affair : he spoke sometimes of 'the starved romance of my life'.
Perhaps he intentionally removed all traces of any amorous
intrigue, or perhaps he did indeed flee any intimate contact
with women. The most that is known is that he was attracted
to them, that he enjoyed long and affectionate friendships with
such socialites and literary figures as Fanny Kemble, Mrs
Greville, Mrs Humphrey Ward, Mrs Elizabeth Boott and Mrs
Katherine Bronson.

His unique emotional relationship (as Leon Edel has shown)

was with the little-known American novelist Constance Fenimore Cooper, the niece of James Fenimore Cooper and author
of *Castle Nowhere*, *Anne*, *East Angels* and other works. It
lasted for about fifteen years. An expatriate like James, she
lived for the most part in Florence and in Oxford; she suffered
from deafness; this accounted perhaps for the loneliness and
the melancholy that surrounded her, and also possibly for her
somewhat withdrawn attitude as far as James was concerned—
the ambiguous way in which she expressed her feelings for him.
She was a fervent admirer of his writings, but often accused
him of inadequately portraying the female heart and true love.
James' kind though non-committal attention to her made her
undoubtedly more unhappy than happy, but she appears to
have persisted in an illusory hope. He always spoke of her with
respect, calling her 'an excellent and sympathetic being', 'a
very good woman with an immense power of devotion (to
H.J.!)' [*sic*], 'the gentlest and kindest of women—and to me
an admirable friend'. He experienced and showed affection,
although without ever exceeding his natural aloofness; Miss
Cooper's death (everything would seem to indicate that she
committed suicide) upset him deeply and caused him lasting
regret and remorse. That they had destroyed by mutual agreement all the letters exchanged between them would indicate
the closeness of their friendship. Even if it never grew into
physical intimacy, it was one of the rare occasions on which
James tried to escape from his usual egotism and to seek—as
far as this was possible for him—a relationship that was, in
his own words, 'extremely intimate'.

By 1880 James had achieved more extensive literary fame
and had devoted himself entirely to his work; to him writing
was a profession, not only because he was an artist aware of his
art, but also because he wished to be independent and live by
his pen. At this time his belief developed that the true artist cannot experience personal happiness, since it would restrain his
creative spirit. In London he led an active social life, and soon
became an indispensable presence in the various drawing-
rooms and clubs that he visited. He was a guest of Lord Rose-

bery, Lady Playfair, Ferdinand de Rothschild, the Archbishop of Canterbury, the Duchess of Sutherland, to mention only a few of his illustrious acquaintances. Little by little, his solitude and detachment lessened in these surroundings and he gained a reputation as a voluble and original conversationalist.

Nevertheless, he was not taken in by the social world and its frivolity, being always careful to keep at a distance and safeguard the prerogatives of his art. He sometimes felt he was overdoing sociability, became weary and bored, wanted to 'get away from the London crowd, the London hubub, all the entanglements and interruptions of London life. . . .' He bought Lamb House, at Rye, Sussex, where he lived in relative seclusion, although he frequently entertained his friends there, with somewhat ceremonious hospitality. But he took a real interest in the literary events and the writers of his time : he had met Ruskin and William Morris, George Eliot and Tennyson; among his close associates were Robert Browning, Meredith, R. L. Stevenson, and Edmund Gosse; later he came to know George Moore, Rudyard Kipling, Joseph Conrad, H. G. Wells, and at the turn of the century, he expressed his sympathy with the new literary generation—young writers turned to him for advice and criticism. On the other hand, he remained an indefatigable traveller, going almost every year to France, Italy and sometimes Germany. In Paris he visited his French acquaintances, whom he also entertained occasionally in London : the novelists Paul Bourget and Alphonse Daudet above all; and in Italy he would go to Florence and Venice, where he met many of his expatriate American friends.

In his own lifetime Henry James did not enjoy the renown, and even popularity, that he believed he deserved; with the exception of *Daisy Miller*, his books did not sell well, and his readers, though faithful, were rather of the selective, connoisseur type. After having spent thirty years publishing stories, long tales and novels, near 1890 he turned to the theatre with the hope of reaching a wider public. His 'dramatic years' (L. Edel) were to be terminated by a rejection which persuaded him to withdraw further into himself and give free rein to his own way of feeling and writing. This was the birth of the 'major phase' (F. O. Matthiessen), the period of a series of powerful masterpieces written in rapid succession, which no less encountered the apathy of the public.

During the Great War, James witnessed with deep concern the disintegration of the civilized world in which he had chosen to live; as if to affirm with a final gesture his attachment to a Europe torn by suffering and sacrifice, he became a naturalized British subject—at the age of seventy-two. He died in London the following year—February 28, 1916—after two heart attacks. According to his own wish, his body was returned to America for burial in the family plot of the Mount Auburn cemetery, Cambridge, Massachusetts.

## 2. From the Man to his Work

A PSYCHOLOGICAL portrait of Henry James is not easily drawn. He would seem never to have offered his contemporaries a direct, frank image of his personality; his letters and *Notebooks* are sometimes more elusive than revealing—despite the rich flow of style.

Even James' physical appearance is reconstructed with difficulty. With his clearly defined, classical features—determined chin, heavy and expressive lips, inquiring, penetrating and slightly sad eyes—he possessed, according to Edmund Gosse, an altogether bold and striking look. He had, however, changing, contrasting expressions which conveyed the belief that he was several persons at the same time; and his somehow exotic, outlandish manner made him seem more Latin than English or American. His friends have compared him successively to a romantic actor, an admiral and a Jewish banker; some saw him as a French divine or man of letters—a Lacordaire or a Sainte-Beuve.

His distinguished bearing and manners were those of a gentleman of his time, but his reserve placed him in a distinct category: 'His manner was grave, extremely courteous,' Gosse said, 'but a little formal and frightened, which seemed strange in a man living in constant communication with the world'. Behind the worldly charm and the reticent attitude was the real man: likeable and good, devoted and sincere, modest and even shy. In 1889, his brother William protrayed him as follows: 'Harry is as nice and simple and amiable as he can be. He has covered himself like some marine crustacean, with all sorts of material growths, rich sea-weeds and rigid barnacles

14

and things, and lives hidden in the midst of his strange heavy alien manners and customs; but these are all but "protective resemblances", under which the same, dear, old, good, innocent and at bottom very powerless-feeling Harry remains, caring for little but his writing, and full of dutifulness and affection for all gentle things.'

Those who have tried to describe James have always stressed the duality of his nature, distinguishing between his apparent and his secret life : the external attitude, without necessarily being affected, served as a protection, a persona covering a reality within him, more true though unexpressed. Constance Fenimore Cooper wrote to him : 'The best part of you is your incorruptible and dignified and reasonable modesty and your perfectly balanced common sense', and James saw himself as 'a very sentient and affectionate albeit out-of-the-way and out-of-the-fashion person'.

There is a well-established critical tradition that the essential personality and private life of James pose a problem and contain an almost insoluble mystery; beyond environmental influences, family or education, one speculates on the possible effects of his 'accident' on his intimate life—that he did not lead. But to seek thus at all costs an answer, would inevitably set James in one of the psycho-sexual behaviour-patterns to which modern psychology has accustomed us and which, like many deterministic hypotheses, might be equally erroneous and correct. It is not certain that, after having defined his tendencies, drawn up a list of his close relationships, supposed such and such anomaly or even the absence of any anomaly, doubts would be gone and an unquestionable truth would emerge. In James' case, an admission that not everything is known or knowable, would seem to be the sole tenable basis for understanding him. Concerning life and human nature, he himself has continually demonstrated that there are no easy, simplified delimitations; that one faces an obscure and contradictory totality, bonds and connexions between various polarities, approximations that *suggest* a fluctuating reality deeply felt rather than proven literal and factual evidences. It would be pointless to mention an aberration (sexual or any other kind) in the case of James, even after admitting that it could have existed; for not the aberration as such would be important, but his attitude toward it and the use he made of it for himself, i.e. the invisible connexion implying a venture of higher scope, regarding life and spirit—his search for a moral identity and his artistic creation. Like many men and with as many reasons, James found difficulty in understanding who he was and what his individual rôle entailed; his non-determined orientations, his modulating process, his quest for possible answers constitute an effort of self-knowledge, less apparent in his personality as the world saw it, than in his tormented sense of art. For him, his work was ultimately the most powerful and satisfying form of affirmation. After his many hesitations with respect to love (whatever his own direction might have been) he treated the subject with a greater ease toward the end of his life, but this audacity (whether the reason be the more permissive influences of the age or his own increasing assurance in emotional life), was a more intellectual liberation, rather disconnected from experience; once again it confirmed his inability—in this area as in another—to express his desires in action and his preference to see them as occurrences of sensitivity and mind. James' personality, like those of his characters, does not follow any positive dictates, only a free interplay of secret idiosyncrasies and gradually revealing factors. Whatever definitions emerge provisionally, they should encompass an amount of mystery of unknowable possibilities to be discovered : there is no final word or conclusion about the individual tendencies and private life of Henry James.

His psychology was above all withdrawn and indrawn : for he could never cross the road that led from the self to its expression in the world. This stemmed partly from conflicts and repressions undergone in his youth, sickness and timidity, his feeling of inadequacy and 'otherness'—various aspects of which appear converted in the prism of his fiction. But in appearance only he had an unstable and passive identity : He was as sociable as circumstances demanded; his integrity of character,

his readiness to oblige were above reproach; and his energy
for work was immense. However, his intrinsic solitude was innate and incurable, for it arose from his inner doubts as well
as a tension with his environment; it eventually set him apart
and, as a writer, made him a witness of and to the passions and
fates of others. His inability to rely more closely on experience
was transformed into the power to imagine and to analyse with
intensity. He accepted the consequences of his situation, his
destiny as 'that queer monster, the artist, an obstinate finality,
an exhaustible sensibility.'

Several critics have stated that James' art is not truly based
on life, because the facts described would appear to have come
to him at second hand : he was convinced from the start that
a deep involvement was also possible through indirect participation in other peoples' adventures and pursuits. On the other
hand, he seems unable to cope with certain aspects of reality,
practical or physical, cruel or ugly, and if he succeeds it is with
innumerable precautions, by an imaginative, poetical transposition and purification, which, at the same time, blurs reality.
Charles Du Bos has said that 'it is the fear of life that is central
. . . in his works, . . . a fear, in excessive humility, of approaching the subject which he would nevertheless like to speak of'.
And Percy Lubbock writes in his excellent introduction to
James' *Letters* : '[He] spoke of himself as a confirmed specta-
tor, one who looked on from the brink instead of plunging on
his own account; but if this seemed a pale substitute for direct
contact he knew very well that it was a much richer and more
adventurous life, really, than it is given to most people to lead.'

This particular attitude has turned James into a prominent
analytical writer. He prefers to probe for what remains hidden
in the external framework and in human behaviour, not content to consider them at their face value and merely describe
them. He multiplies the number of observing angles and approaches to such an extent that in his writings life appears to
be less lived than analysed and felt in so many slowly revelatory stages. The representation is not necessarily abstract, for
the author is careful not to dissociate it from the reality it

expresses, but rather to underline the organic essential points of the relationship between interpretation and subject matter. In fact his very withdrawal from appearances, the superficial forms of life, is the result of his wish to attain a more immutable reality. For James, 'The novelist is a particular window' opened onto the world; he should simultaneously 'intensely consult and intensely ignore life'. His own inspiration is derived from vivid, immediate impressions, but once they are received, he cultivates them alone : i.e. estranged to the source which brought them to him. 'Initially,' wrote Du Bos, 'it is a faint breeze conveyed to him by life . . . a breeze of which he wishes to know no more, so strong is his belief that life can only be marred by amplification.' James' creative process is one of strict selection. From reality he wishes to draw merely the most significant essence, what he calls the 'germ' : given that, he can enclose the maximum intensity within the minimum of space. The reason for the decreasing number of events in his novels is his desire to create an increasingly powerful aura of tension.

James tries to examine the *relation* between people and between people and things in particular situations, rather than to see them in their innate value as general and unchangeable. He does not present a series of isolated events and impressions, for 'each of them is seen by virtue of the rays of light shed upon it by all the others'. (Ch. du Bos.) Like the hero of *The Princess Casamassima*, James has a 'rather helpless sense, that, whatever he saw, he saw—and this was always the case—so many other things besides'. He always places an imaginative halo about his actual subjects and adds deeper implications; landscapes, events or objects are no longer merely displayed but are endowed with inner light and meaning. Like a painter—like Manet, who at that time made similar and radical changes in the artist's attitude to reality—James strives above all to express a *relationship*—*his* relationship with the world. As he himself wrote, 'a novel is, in its broadest definition, a personal, a direct impression of life'.

James lived with greater power on a plane different from that of external circumstances and easily felt emotions; although by choice not a man of action, he knew how—deliberately, whenever his art demanded it—to 'intensely ignore life'. His artistic universe overflowed with closely-packed associations and perceptions to which he applied his unceasing intuition and discernment, relegating nothing to oblivion without having first exhausted all its evocative substance: his family's old habit of always converting everything into inner moral trials found its most masterful purpose here. For James, as for André Malraux, it was necessary to transform into 'conscientiousness the greatest possible extent of experience', even though the experience remained within. 'There was no hour,' said Percy Lubbock, 'in which he was not alive with the whole of his sensibility; he could scarcely persuade himself that he might have had time for more.' James himself, protesting against the banal views generally held of life and reality, wrote : 'Of course, for myself I live, live intensely and am fed by life, and my value whatever it be, is my own kind of expression of that'.

Able to live only by observing life within the enclosed world of his mental existence, James embarked on his analytical presentation of reality as on a liberation of the self, gradually resolving the doubts and inadequacies imposed upon him since childhood, changing his passivity into perceptive intensity, and thus, finally—through his original creations—participating in life again. He had felt in himself 'the power to neglect something thoroughly', to be free 'to abound aggressively in his own sense and express without reserve his own saturation.' 'My *work*,' he said, 'is my salvation.'

\*     \*

James' literary career has three phases. His early stories, often romantic in fashion, with supernatural and fantastic elements, are concerned with the Civil War and life in New England; they are uneven in merit, for the young author is still trying his hand at different styles and subjects, under the influence of the novelists whom he admires : Hawthorne and Turgenev, George Sand and George Eliot, Merimée and Balzac. Certain tendencies already reappear : above all he is in the process of gradually forsaking the American environment and turning to the representation of his compatriots in Europe. This is the particular stage of his 'international theme', which he will never completely abandon.

During his mature years, from 1880 on, James extended his work in various directions and especially devoted himself to writing some elaborate social novels. These works have not yet the close-knit structure of those that follow, but they evidence an order free from inessentials, of a clear and finely balanced style. James gains ground, appears more as an arresting and powerful novelist. From 1890 to 1895, 'lacking public esteem', he undertook writing for the theatre : only *Guy Domville* can be praised as an interesting and convincing play.

After the setbacks of these years, James' work enters its final and most brilliant phase. He adroitly applies theatrical technique to a series of short novels on the one hand, and brings new life to the short story by his clever subjects and artistry on the other. In the great novels of his last years, he develops anew with unusual power the central themes of his fiction, and a truly original mastery of 'the expanding consciousness' and a richly symbolic style.

James tried all literary forms with the exception of poetry. He wrote art criticism, theatrical studies and plays, published travel reminiscences[1] and memoirs.[2] His early articles, his essays, concerned primarily with European writers[3] and, above all, the prefaces to his Collected Edition, entitle him to be called an important literary critic and theoretician of his time. His most valuable contribution, however, was in the realm of the short story, the long tale and the novel : he was an experimental novelist whose originality never failed him and who introduced new concepts and techniques in the art of fiction.

Before discussing the works themselves and the major themes, a word should be said about their most general character. The elements of the Jamesian universe, when reduced to bare out-

---

[1] *A Little Tour in France*, 1884; *The American Scene*, 1907, and others.
[2] *A Small Boy and Others*, 1913; *Notes of a Son and a Brother*, 1914.
[3] *French Poets and Novelists*, 1878; *Partial Portraits*, 1888, and others.

lines, often appear grotesque and extraordinary, for they are magnified by imagination : he drew his inspiration from life as he observed it, but his subjects were of interest to him only on account of their plastic and moral contents. There are no romantic and descriptive aspects : nothing is perceived in terms of plot or as a series of events : the development is principally psychological. This is why James' works are extremely difficult to summarize; their value lies less in the framework and in the story than in the overall atmosphere and the successive spiritual states of the heroes.

These heroes strike us as being unreal, disembodied, since they live more in a world of inner thought and tensions than in the real world. Even when they are well delineated, we always know their impulses, motivations, feelings, better than their acts. Almost all of them conceive of a somewhat narrow pursuit of individual well-being, and their loves, fortune-hunting and travels can hardly be substitutes for commitment to life. They belong to no social group and no professional category; they acknowledge no ideological conviction; solely preoccupied with themselves, they seek self-knowledge instead of happiness and worldly purpose.

James' ambition was to be a realist and portray the life and conditions of his times, but he only succeeded in describing best the privileged society in which he lived—a leisured class of American expatriates and a cosmopolitan European aristocracy. The conventional and the decorous held for him a real attraction, and he never freed himself from the tenuous atmosphere of Victorian drawing-room niceties and correctness. Although this representation sometimes may seem irrelevant, concerned with affected values and not the harsh realities of daily existence, it is far from being superficial or being admired without reserve : in this environment, James showed the corruption of modern manners and the decadence of social standards; on the other hand, he also saw in it—thanks to the individual's reactions and exposure to foreign ways and old cultures—the means of attaining to a supreme refinement of beauty and of behaviour.

Another constant feature of his work is his practice of never openly stating the moral problem under examination. There are no reflections and generalizations in his prose narratives; he analyses men and life without judging them, discovering himself, step by step, their ultimate significance. The nature of his subjects—always seen at the progressive stages of an increasing knowledge—remains closely linked to a technique that preserves the tension of its efforts to seek deeper revelations. The effect of the works is always in their reverberations suggested and psychological hints. And so it is difficult to quote passages explicit in themselves or representative of a particular development: James' true style is a style in transition.

In short, it is possible to reproach James for a lack of a more extensive social vision and a more direct expression. But these limitations, partly the results of his life and character, he transformed into artistic qualities, psychological inquiry and portrayals of inner reality. Whatever the subject-matter he chose to develop, he always explored the areas behind mere appearances and attitudes; his works are an attempt to describe man's conflict with himself and with the world.

# 3. America—Europe

PERHAPS HENRY JAMES would have been able to live and write in the country in which he was born, for he was convinced that 'the face of nature and civilization in this our country is to a certain point a very sufficient literary field. But it will yield its secret only to a really grasping imagination.' He himself possessed this imaginative power—to such an extent however that he could never be satisfied with American innocence and material well-being: they appeared devoid of true drama, social clashes or personal conflicts. He writes at length of the simple character of his fellow-countrymen, of 'the simple social order from across the sea;' and with marked preference he opposes them to 'the complex social machinery,' to the 'denser, richer, warmer European spectacle;' according to him, there must be 'such an accumulation of history and customs, such complexity of manners and types, to form a fund of suggestion for a novelist'.

James was well aware of the special position of the United States, which had not yet developed its own civilization and, despite its distinct new features, was still too dependent on Europe: 'It's a complex fate being an American, and one of the responsibilities it entails is fighting against a superstitious valuation of Europe'. He took some pride in the possibilities before an America whose sights were entirely on the future and which could fashion for man the promise of better conditions and of higher understanding. 'We are American born . . . I look upon it as a great blessing; and I think that to be an American is an excellent preparation for culture. We have exquisite qualities as a race, and it seems to be that we are

ahead of the European races in the fact that more than either
of them, we can deal freely with forms of civilization not our
own. . . . We must of course have something of our own—
something distinctive and homogeneous—and I take it that we
shall find it in our moral consciousness, our unprecendental
spiritual lightness and vigour.' In his cosmopolitan episodes,
James was not merely concerned with travel and adventure,
rather with the present and future state of maturity of his
country—the relation of Americanism with stronger foreign
standards and the conflict thus created—where it could be
finally destroyed or confirmed. He lived this problem himself :
the question of whether a cultured American does not always
feel an inadequacy in respect to life and civilization, and, to a
certain extent, is condemned to be an expatriate. Actual resi-
dence abroad is not an absolute physical necessity; it is only
the symbolic image of this social and spiritual exile.

.The characters of his novels are 'arranged, gathered for a
performance, the performance of Europe', and will never
escape this condition. To the end, they remain spectators of
their own dilemma, never determining the choice or the action
that would bring them the practical solutions—and the illusions
—they seek. Neither Europeans nor Americans, they are as if
suspended, excluded, denied, alone—in search of moral forti-
tude and aesthetic vibrations, rather than a national identity.
'If we're not good Americans,' one of them freely admits,
'we're certainly poor Europeans; we've no national place here.
We're mere parasites, crawling over the surface; we haven't
our feet in the soil.'

In abandoning the purely American subjects, James strives
with his 'international theme', to stage the meeting of America
and Europe. In certain stories Europe is no more than the basis
of a picturesque setting—a kind of travelogue offering amusing
encounters and impressive sites; in others, a real conflict is
established between the Americans and the Europeans. The first
personify love for life, innocence and honesty, whereas the
latter represent a complex society, fraught with mysteries and
contradictions. Only from the moment when James opposes

their different conceptions of life (on the social level only, in his early narratives), does he discover the real possibilities of his topic. In the light and humorous novel *The Europeans* (1878), for once the Europeans travel to the New World. Baroness Munster and her brother Felix, are American by origin but inveterate cosmopolitans, 'foreigners of some sort': the Baroness, 'a sophisticated mind', has acquired all the pretences and prejudices of European worldliness, while Felix sees himself in the rôle of 'adventurer', 'artist' and 'bohemian', having visited the cities of Europe haphazardly as an itinerant painter, violinist and actor. Debilitated and short of money, having exhausted better chances and hopes, they both come to seek their fortune in the family of Mr Wentworth, their exceedingly rich uncle. What do they find in New England? 'The simple, serious life' of their hosts: 'It's primitive; it's patriarchal; it's the *ton* of the golden age. . . . They are sober; they are even severe. They are of a pensive cast; they take things harsh. I think there is something the matter with them; they have some melancholy memory or some depressing expectation.' In this prosaic environment, the Baroness and Felix are universally admired for their showy, pretentious manners which the small provincial town deems to be of the best of tastes; they create a grand impression and seem able to obtain whatever they desire: riches or a good match. But the Wentworths, despite their good-natured disposition, fear some danger. . . . 'We must all be careful', they tell each other. 'This is a great change; we are to be exposed to peculiar influences.' James, not without irony, portrays their innocence as incorruptible to the extent that they can never discern the devious schemes of their guests:' all the stratagems of the Baroness are wasted on them. Her vanity wounded, she leaves America. The personality of Felix is more flexible, he is ready to accept whatever chance may bring: 'I don't think it's what one does or one doesn't do that promotes enjoyment . . .' he cheerfully says. 'It is the general way of looking at life.' His way is to seek liberty and wide experience: having fallen in love with his cousin Gertrude Wentworth, he promised her happiness, adventure, Europe. . . . The narrative ends with their marriage.

The interest of the novel is neither in the plot nor in the characters' psychology, but in the depiction of the two social groups. James deliberately exaggerates his effects, and his method here verges almost on caricature : the puritan simplicity of the Americans and the eccentric snobbery of the Europeans are possibly over-emphasized. The novel contains a number of realistic, comic sketches, charming and truthful. Nevertheless, as a whole, the work is only partly successful; by restricting himself to the study of differences in manners, James decidedly reduces the dramatic impact.

In his other works, he assumes the point of view of the individual, and it is now the Americans who visit Europe. A conflict is possible on this basis : faced with an unbending and complex social order, with old traditions and cultures, they feel out of place, are often criticized and misjudged; above all they suffer, and through suffering, they change. These travellers are quite varied. Among the less important ones, often amusing figures, are adventurers eager for riches or millionaires on holiday, journalists or second-rate painters, and many ordinary tourists. The main characters, on the other hand, constitute a serious group of tormented artists, retired business men, fair young women who want to learn all about life. . . .

In several early works, James studies the expatriate American artist and his lonely struggles abroad. The hero of *The Madonna of the Future* (1873), (a story which recalls Balzac's *Un Chef-d'oeuvre inconnu*), has left America because : 'Our crude and garish climate, our silent past, our deafening present, the constant pressure about us of unlovely circumstance, are as void of all that nourishes and prompts and inspires the artist, as my sad heart is void of bitterness in saying so ! We poor aspirants must live in perpetual exile.' Established at Florence, he spends his life admiring the museums and Madonnas of the past and in studying his model (a beautiful signora), so that someday he may paint a pure work of art—the Madonna of the Madonnas. But the years pass and he realizes too late that his striving for perfection was a vain illusion : his model is now an old woman and he has missed everything. He dies in his miserable lodging, leaving on the easel 'a canvas that was a mere dead blank, cracked and discoloured by time'—the projected masterpiece that he had never begun.

James's first novel, *Roderick Hudson* (1875), presents the moral, 'most unexpected failure' of Roderick, a talented young American sculptor who has come to work in Rome's more congenial, inspiring surroundings; there his gifts are gradually destroyed by his dissipated life and his love for Christina Light. 'I don't understand so much power . . . going with so much weakness, such a brilliant gift being subject to such lapses . . .' complains his patron and friend Rowland. 'Roderick's standard is immensely high; I must do him that justice. He'll do nothing beneath it, and while he's waiting for the vision to descend, his imagination, his nerves, his senses must have something to amuse them. . . .' Deserted by Christina, who marries someone else, Roderick steadily declines and neglects his art. Having come to Italy to discover a greater sense of beauty and to create his best work, he is now at a standstill, discouraged and alone : 'I shall never be anything again; it's no use talking! But I don't know what secret spring has been touched since I've lain here. Something in my heart seems suddenly to open and let in a flood of beauty and desire. I know what I've lost and I think it horrible.' He escapes from Rome, goes to Switzerland, and kills himself in an Alpine crevasse.

The novel is romantic in tone and not very convincing. The interest resides in the Italian framework, in the precise colourful notations of people, monuments and places. As in *The Madonna of the Future*, James does not succeed in creating here a real dramatic confrontation between the artist and Europe : Roderick's decline and suffering are not strongly conveyed, and the reader finds little justification for the pernicious influence of the Old World—supposedly corrupt and superficial, despite its grand tradition of art and glory.

The conflict experienced by Newman, in *The American*

(1877), seems more true, although with certain traces of melo-drama. This 'powerful specimen of an American', 'a self-made practical man' and a 'born experimentalist', is 'frank' and 'simple as a little child'; his personality reflects assuredness and he naïvely admires all he does : 'I have a very good opinion of myself,' he says. At thirty-six, his fortune made, he decides to travel to Europe. A more or less conventional comic tourist type, he is the 'great Western Barbarian' coming to civilization, eager to see and understand everything, but only impressed by gross material factors—the tremendous size and old age of châteaux and cathedrals. In Paris, he orders from Mlle Nioche (who applies her meagre talents to copying the works of the Masters) reproductions of the largest paintings in the Louvre. 'He believed that Europe was made for him, and not he for Europe.' 'I want the biggest kind of entertainment a man can get, people, places, art, nature, everything! I want to see the tallest mountains, and the bluest lakes, and the finest pictures, and the handsomest churches, and the most celebrated men, and the most beautiful women.' Europe, however, can hardly teach him anything, for he lacks insight and is unable to feel the finer presences of the past. 'The complex Parisian world about him seemed a very simple affair; it was an immense, amazing spectacle, but it neither inflamed his imagination nor irritated his curiosity.'

He meets Countess Claire de Cintré, a young widow, 'half a *grande dame* and half an angel', who falls in love with him and whom he intends to marry. But her family, the Bellegardes, after having consented suddenly change their attitude and no longer approve of Newman; they do not think, after all, that Claire could marry a business man, even if he is a millionaire —and they find a more suitable partner for her. Outraged by such malevolent and disdainful conduct, Newman tries to coerce them, threatening to reveal (and he has the written proof) the murder committed in the family a few years earlier. Claire, thwarted in her search for happiness, retreats to a con-vent and becomes a Carmelite nun. Newman then abandons all thought of vengeance : having lost all desire to become part of this world of 'prejudices' and 'traditions', he chooses to return to America for good.

There are many easily contrived incidents and unrealistic effects in the book. As in *The Europeans*, James sometimes oversimplifies the national psychologies in order to emphasize the differences between Americans and Europeans: the Bellegardes, with their arrogance and moral cruelty, with their 'mean and underhand behaviour', are too darkly drawn. Varied descriptions of Parisian life underline the inflexibility of the social order and the omnipotence of the family; these forces are ranged against the young and their right to be happy: Valentin de Bellegrade has himself killed in a duel; Claire takes the veil, the young marquise will never free herself from conventionality; and Mlle Nioche, for want of a better chance in life, is doomed to prostitution.

In this world of 'tolerably depraved' Parisians, ruled by intrigues and vanity, ultimately Newman appears more noble in his candour and generosity. He is the first Jamesian hero for whom the experience of Europe is tantamount to change and refinement of character. '. . . This horrible Paris hardens one's heart', Valentin says to him, 'but it quickens one's wits, and it ends by teaching one a refinement of observation.' Newman loses, as far as happiness is concerned, but he gains on the moral plane, reaffirming his honest, simple Americanism. According to the preface, the culmination of his venture is that he would 'suffer at the hands of persons pretending to represent the highest possible civilization. . . . All he would have at the end . . . will be just the moral convenience, indeed the moral necessity, of his practical but quite unappreciated, magnanimity. . . .'

Subsequently, the crisis experienced by the American in Europe will be similar to Newman's and increasingly emphasized. In his succeeding novels, James chooses more successful main characters: he prefers the figure of a young American woman, beautiful and rich, impatient to live, but rather naïve about the ways of the world and European society, where she is soon subjected to exploitation and misunderstanding. She meets with love, she moves in an atmosphere of elegance and historical beauty, but she learns about the trials of suffering and sacrifice.

James devoted several works to this idealized, pure, and sensitive American heroine. Among them was *Daisy Miller* (1878), which brought him fame. Daisy is an 'American girl of so pronounced a type', 'extremely innocent' and 'very unsophisticated', 'charming, but how deucedly sociable' : she is 'only a pretty American flirt' and means 'no harm'. In Rome, where she spends a winter with her mother and teen-age brother (both quite eccentric and rather indifferent to her) she is attracted by the novelty of her experience, people and places; she looks for amusement and excitement, enjoys the company of Giovanelli—a man of poor reputation, but kind to her. She does 'everything that is not done here', comments a prudish Roman lady. 'Flirting with any man she could pick up ! sitting in corners with mysterious Italians; dancing all the evening with the same partners; receiving visits at eleven o'clock at night.' Roman society condemns and shuns her, but Daisy cares little about scandalous gossip; sure of herself, of her purity and good intentions, she is not ready to submit to hypocrisy and conventions : 'I, thank goodness, am not a young lady of this country,' she proclaims, 'I don't see why I should change my habits for *them*.' Exasperated by the 'injustice' of the Romans, she wishes further to explore her freedom of action; she goes from excess to excess, contracts malaria and dies.

The portrait of Daisy is acute and vivid, although she appears hardly conscious of the deep tensions and implications of her plight; her death is more of an accident than a symbolic martyrdom. In her, James has personified innocence and independence—American innocence and independence—and the right of every individual to live as he sees fit; Daisy is guilty only of doing what she wants, but narrow-minded society is more guilty for judging her, and judging her according to her external attitudes rather than her intrinsic nature. A victim of European bourgeois morality, she triumphs only in the memory of Winterbourne, a young American expatriate who loved her without declaring his love, and who is now the only one—even though too late—to understand Daisy's wasted youth and pure spontaneity.

*The Reverberator* (1888) is another example of a comparative study of a young American woman and a group of conformist Europeans. Francie, the heroine, is not welcome in the family of her French fiancé, Gaston Probert, since quite innocently, without ill intention, she has spoken to an American newsman about certain dishonourable secrets of the Proberts. Now, she refuses to deny (as they request) what she has inadvertently revealed and knows to be true: she wants to be accepted as she is. Faced with prejudice and intransigence, she achieves a kind of heroism in affirming her distaste for hypocritical compromises. As in the case of Newman, the experience of Europe makes her conscious of her personality, of her probity and her moral strength.

James gives his 'international theme' an even wider range of psychological innuendoes in *The Portrait of a Lady* (1881) and *The Wings of the Dove* (1902). European society is no longer described in few brisk, disparaging outlines, and the Americans are not merely opposed to the Europeans in an oversimplified contrast of national features. In these two novels, James submits the respective heroines to a profound, tormented self-knowledge in the face of renunciation and solitude. Different from the type represented by Daisy, they are more intelligent and intuitive, more responsible and ambitious, and they do not lay themselves open to the reproaches of the Europeans; their souls imprisoned by an idealized vision of the Old World, they realize too late that their good faith and innocence have been abused by their European *friends*, that they must abandon all hope of personal satisfaction and joy, devoid of social aspect. Their involvement is not social but an intimate tragedy which they live with intensity: it transcends the international confrontation, and the retribution they seek is on a higher level. They will recur in another context.

In *The Ambassadors* (1903), considered by many to be James' masterpiece, Europe assumes the function of a charac-

ter. Thanks to the hero's ability to convert his varied contacts
abroad into moral experience, the conflict between Europe
and the Americans results in a synthesis. When he arrives in
Paris, late in life, with the sense that he has waited too long and
missed much, Louis Lambert Strether is concerned with
Europe above all else : it captivates him and causes him to turn
aside from the objectives of his trip. He has been sent to repatri-
ate Chad, the son of his rich widowed fiancée, Mrs Newsome;
the extremely puritan Newsomes are convinced that the young
man is leading a dissolute life in Paris and that a fast woman
is preventing him from returning back home. But Strether
meets an unexpectedly new Chad : not a loose liver but a
gentleman of culture who belongs to the best artistic and aristo-
cratic circles. And the women whom the Newsomes had
imagined to be vulgar creatures turn out to be the Comtesse
de Vionnet, exquisite and of noble character, and her sixteen-
year-old daughter.

Gradually, Strether comes to understand Chad, to admire
his privileged life, and abandons the plan to make him leave
for America. The distant but tyrannical Mrs Newsome thinks
that he has gone over to the enemy and sends more resolute
emissaries : her daughter Mrs Pocock, her son-in-law Jim and
the young Mamie, whom she has chosen for Chad. In Paris,
Mrs Pocock finds everything suspicious and immoral; Jim can
hardly imagine what it is all about, but Mamie is perceptive
enough to make out Chad's situation and to realize that she
will not do for him. Having failed in their mission, they all
return to America.

Strether, typically American in his way of seeing things as
better and simpler than they actually are, believes Chad to be
in love with Mlle de Vionnet and only later does he discover
him to be really the mother's lover. At the same time he finds
out that, on one hand, the young man is tiring of the affair and
perhaps could decide to leave the country after all, and on the
other, that Mme de Vionnet is still passionately in love with
him. Slowly, Strether accepts and sinks deeper in this complex
and tenuous relationship, indentifying himself in turn with

each partner's predicament; having also failed in the original purpose of his journey, he definitely breaks with Mrs Newsome and stops corresponding with her. He feels more and more an obligation toward Mme de Vionnet, to whom he is increasingly attracted, and whom he knows to be unhappy. For her sake he now wants to persuade Chad to remain in Paris; but ultimately, he will not have achieved anything positive and saved the two lovers' future. As for himself, no longer can he expect to marry Mrs Newsome; he refuses the possibility of close ties with Miss Gostrey, a travelling American journalist; he is unable to declare his secret love for Mme de Vionnet. . . . He appears to have lost everything. Requiring no reward for his sympathy, for his sacrifices, he chooses to return to America, alone.

Strether's mission has developed in an unexpected direction, because Europe has conquered him; many of his hopes have been ruined through his venture, but he has gained, and gained considerably. For him, Paris is not the city that Christopher Newman experienced in *The American*; it is a brilliant cluster of incitements to beauty, refinement and stronger emotions : 'The cup of his impressions seemed truly to overflow'; from all sides there came to him 'the vague voice of Paris. Strether had all along been subject to sudden gusts of fancy . . . odd starts of the historic sense, suppositions and divinations with no warrant but their intensity'. In presence of this 'new scale of relations', he discovers a 'finer taste' in living, but more than anyone else Mme de Vionnet, with her 'general high-pitched essence', '. . . comes . . . to stand . . . for most of the things that make the *charm* of civilization'. 'Her charm is independent of [love] for him, and gratifies some more distinctively disinterested aesthetic, intellectual, social, even, so to speak, historic sense in him, which has never yet been *a pareille fête*, never found itself so called to the front.' At fifty-five, aware that he has failed (being in America the editor of an obscure provincial periodical), he acquires in Europe within the span of a few months a belated sense of youth and freedom, the sense of having lived to the full. His destiny seems to have spread suddenly before him: 'Of course, I'm youth—youth for the trip to Europe . . . I'm making up late for what I didn't have early. I cultivate my little benefit in my own little way. It amuses me more than anything that has happened to me in all my life. They may say what they like—it's my surrender, it's my tribute, to youth. One puts that in where one can—it has to come in somewhere, if only out of the lives, the conditions, the feelings of other persons. Chad gives me the sense of it . . . and she does the same. . . . Yes, they're my youth; since somehow, at the right time, nothing else ever was. What I meant just now therefore is that it would all go—go before doing its work—if they were to fail me.'

In *The Ambassadors*, we find the most complete expression of what Europe has come to mean for James and for his heroes. In his previous works, he frequently finds fault with continental society, its exclusiveness, prejudices, corruption: it seems to have reached a point of immobility, lacking henceforth decency and real strength. The European characters are less honourable, attractive, and next to the Americans, they most often assume the part of villains; in the case of the Bellegardes and the Proberts, respectability hides more than one vice: lies, adultery, theft and even murder. But in his later novels, James' vision has developed considerably; Europe has a profound lesson for all the innocents from overseas who ardently search for a new world—'the particular spot in the world which communicates the greatest sense of life'. Prepared by long years of readings, dreams and expectation, they travel in earnest, discovering the delights of an old civilization in 'the presence of new measures, other standards, a different scale of relations'. Their intellects are enriched; they observe and analyse unceasingly; they record in their quickened, feverish imagination the impressions and encounters they are subject to, drawn more particularly to the subtler nuances of art and manners. Faced with trials and tribulations which always end tragically, they are none the less not entirely crushed and vanquished; they have entered a challenging quest for higher gratification and broadened their consciousness of life and of themselves. By means of a paradoxical synthesis, Europe becomes finally the land of freedom where, escaping from their everyday existence and restricted hopes, they see themselves as they really are.

Europe is the mythical *elsewhere* of dreams and poetry to which they secretly aspire—looming in the distance as desirable and promising—where they would resolve the contradictions and limitations of their fate. Europe does not merely stand for *adventure*, but for a journey toward something different and better, something that they have not yet experienced but crave to know, toward a flight from the self and a longing to rediscover the self. Enabled at last to break loose from the standstill and boredom of American realities, they clash with portentous happenings and sacrifices, they come forth with a new sense of liberation into the open field of choice and acceptance. In this way, the international theme of James no longer relies on a contrasting of continents and cultures; this confrontation, not without interest in itself, has found its dramatic counterpart in a psychological crisis and an existential inquiry. In separating the plots, the situations, the individual ordeals from a restrictive social and national environment, and by placing them at a kind of cross-roads or juncture (a more or less abstract juncture), James not only extends the geographical and cultural bounds of his novels but destroys simultaneously the conventional conception of framework or setting. The protagonists seem to exist in a vacuum : they come from nowhere, they are nowhere, they go nowhere. The backcloth is alien and new to them; this particular universe is without dimensions, and fleeting; they neither experience it as an obstacle constraining them, nor as a support which provides stability. In their effort to explain and penetrate its meaning, they encounter only its ever-increasing impenetrability. They have left the world of concrete and comprehensible appearances, have entered one that they can never make their own; they choose to live outside the contingencies which might formulate and justify their presence in the world. Their international involvement represents ultimately a transcendence of external values, of agreements and successes, of the material possessions that they originally wished to acquire; it stands for a point reached upon a route—a point beyond which there lies only self-knowledge and commitment to deeply individual ideals. They came to Europe to see, learn, be happy, take up root in life; they did not know themselves that the security and the satisfactions they seek are not to be found in Europe—as they were not to be found in America. Their national uprooting and general disconnectedness have become a veiled metaphysical quest, Europe representing finally the existence chosen in perfect freedom, to which they alone can give essence by annexing it to their consciousness: in the process they acquired a new moral structure equivalent to a *heightened* sense of *being*, of being *in* the world and fully being *themselves*.

Although James' international subject is judged by several critics to be an inadequate revolt from nineteenth-century realism and a proof of his inability forcefully to delineate a given environment it strikes us as one of his most original qualities, anticipating the twentieth-century novel. In fact, behind the apparent cosmopolitanism, he unmakes the apparent circumambient world so that it no longer has particular specificity, requiring both form and meaning. In Europe, the Jamesian hero is set apart in a more or less vague and hostile dimension that he can neither completely forgo nor master. Therefore, Europe symbolizes the fatal condition which brings him face to face not with what is given, acquired and received, but with the uncertain, the new, the unknown—with that which he must conquer by himself. James is ahead of his times, for he announces a new form of cosmopolitanism where exaltation is far more important than the sensation of exotic escape.

James is not a novelist who delights in travel, adventures, picturesque tourist effects or facile national contrasts. Even if these elements are occasionally encountered in his work, the cosmopolitan vision never becomes an end in itself: it is effective only in relation to the heroes, the extent to which they transcend it or succumb to it. In addition, in preferring to observe existence on the level of Western civilization, James becomes an advocate of a supranational consciousness and the universality of man's fate. He wished to be a writer detached from a national identity and—like his protagonists—to define his creative work not so much in terms of circumstances and environment, as in terms of an experience and a questioning found in no condition other than the human: 'I have not the least hesitation in saying,' he confessed, 'that I aspire to write in such a way that it would be impossible to an outsider to say whether I am at a given moment an American writing about England or an Englishman writing about America (dealing as I do with both countries), and so far from being ashamed of such an ambiguity, I should be exceedingly proud of it, for it would be highly civilized'.

# 4. The Life of an Age

PRIMARILY AN international novelist and a psychologist, James demonstrated an interest in the realist tendencies of French literature and was strongly influenced by such writers as Balzac, Flaubert, Zola and Maupassant. His great ambition to be a novelist of manners was not accidental: 'It is on manners, customs, usages, habits, forms, upon all these things matured and established, that a novelist lives; they are the very stuff his work is made of'. According to James, one could look upon the novel as a form of history and upon the novelist—concerned with accurate observation and direct impressions—as an historian of his own times. In his works, whether the scene is international, American or English, he tends to go beyond the purely individual conditions and describe the broader framework, the typical attitudes of a social group.

After 1880, halfway through his career, he wrote three long novels in the naturalist manner of Zola or of Daudet, and a series of short stories 'à la Maupassant'—in order to 'touch so many subjects, break out in so many places, handle so many of the threads of life'. In addition, in his Collected Works (as Leon Edel has clearly demonstrated) James painstakingly arranged his works in an order reminiscent of Balzac's Comédie Humaine : 'Scenes of the International life', 'Scenes of English Life', 'Scenes of the Life of the Artist', etc., while deliberately omitting works which might be classified as 'Scenes of American Life'. 'I want to leave,' he said, 'a multitude of pictures of my time, projecting my small circular frame upon as many different spots as possible . . . , a total having a certain value as observation and testimony.' The precise notation of detail in his novels concerning America recreate a definite atmosphere : *The Europeans, Washington Square* and *The Bostonians,* for example. James, of course, cannot speak of 'frontier life', the world of business and, in general, economic and social prosperity, but his descriptions of the environment of his youth— provincial mediocrity or the leisured society of New York and of New England—are admirable. His portrayals of place and of character are extremely full; he never reduces American psychology and settings to common, simplified traits; on the whole, his works offer a vivid (though not complete) picture of the American way of life at that time.

James could never free himself from America. Even in his international tales, the moral outlook is always typically and forcefully American; the protagonists can never discard it during their European journeyings. If they are presented in the surroundings of their native country—whatever the bucolic charm or the meagre pleasures—James emphasizes the colourless naïvety, straitness of mind, lack of imagination and of culture, and the increasingly mechanized, commercialized aspects of their existence. But certain selected individuals require release from the milieu in which they are enclosed, wish to be somewhere else—Europe—in order to liberate and to assert themselves. In these eager, tormented heroes, James portrays what he thinks are the strongest, positive American qualities : purity and integrity of character (of which innocent simplicity is sometimes the outward sign); a capacity for wanting persevering and fighting (something of the pioneer's energy transferred to the spiritual plane); a preference for moral values, sympathy and understanding, straightforwardness; a more or less puritan-inspired tendency to condone personal satisfactions and happiness by self-denial and sacrifice. From these finer springs of the American spirit—related to the human ideal implied in the non-conformist origins of the country— James determines the basis for a more open, dynamic and exacting psychology. In fine, James' representation of America is dramatic and contradictory in essence : on the one hand, too simple and uncultured, with a yearning for bad taste and

trivial objectives; on the other, enclosing within its very imperfections a vital hunger for intense life, for the highest personal attainment.

The 'international scene' also relies on direct observation:
its description often plays an important part in the progression
of a given work.

For James, Italy is *the* picturesque setting *per se*: Rome,
Florence and Venice; the sights and cities dear to the tourist;
museums, churches or palaces representing a living accumulation of art and history. This Italy, seen at the end of the nine-
teenth century, is not the land of sun, gaiety and pleasure, but
rather the treasure of the past: the Italy of the Quattrocento
and the baroque era, offering inspiration for a new aestheticism and quest for beauty. This variegated yet stereotyped
backcloth seems detached from the plot, and only occasionally
contributes to the hero's ordeal in Europe. Italy in James'
works is never deeply examined, socially and psychologically
individualized; rather, felt as a totality of notions, exotic
and colourful, artistic and beautiful, it appeals to the imagination.

James' presentation of England and France is far more
detailed. For instance, he reveals less of the general cultural
and architectural riches of Paris and more of the complex
social life which offers the tensions, subtle connexions and
nuances established by a vast tradition. France and Paris are
never examined in terms of their contemporary conflicts and
problems; the evocation, though slightly nebulous, is paradoxic-
ally exact: a perceptive foreigner's sensitivity reacting to the
beauty of an ancient city and to the company of a few people
who, for him, are *the* French. He sees them only as two types:
those corrupted by conformity and prejudices, and those who
personify the refinements of civilization. In the hierarchy of
the Jamesian world, France is most often the quintessence of
Europe which assails the protagonists and becomes the source
of deeper revelations, even when—ultimately—it provokes their
downfall. Except for few well chosen interiors and public
places, the background descriptions are detached from appear-

ances, and increasingly re-oriented toward the intensifying of the psychological drama. They are impressionistic and poetic, rather than factual and picturesque.

England became increasingly important in James' work. With time, he felt more at home in the country, he knew it more intimately, and his ambition was to pass for a purely English author. Somewhat like France, England is often presented as a new and revelatory environment for the innocent travellers from over-seas; there they encounter for the first time the various forms of evil and of sophistication. The 'siege of London' recurs for many a character : for those who seek only worldly success and riches, for those who meet with suffering and disillusion. As they lay seige, they are determined both to triumph and to measure themselves with new standards of perfection. Apparently, James took hardly any interest in contemporary events and conditions in England; he did not examine the family, educational, religious and political structure, or—as a matter of fact—any other practical and pressing aspect of daily life.

The true English content of the novels—apart from the descriptions of places (London and its vicinity, monuments and interiors)—is essentially relative to the behaviour, manners and psychology of a certain wealthy, intellectual class : a tireless pursuit from Hyde Park to five o'clock tea, from stately dinners and receptions to weekend parties in magnificent estates. At times James underlines the cleverness and reserve, distinction and magnanimity, of the English; at times their smallness of mind and egotism, unscrupulous ambition and hypocrisy. This moral anatomy, sensitive and complex, constitutes, the richest and most varied of the several national psychologies James depicts. One finds rarely a recurrence of stereotyped effects or the occasional, somewhat extreme, simplification, of his American and French portrayals are rarely apparent. However, the major import of this examination will be James' gradual stressing of the signs of disorder and disintegration in a brilliant and deceiving world where only the false, the pretentious and the banal persist. He was fascinated, above all, with the con-

trast between the refinements of social life and the accompany-
ing moral decline : in noting the sinister and grotesque disintegration, in substituting for stability and development the idea
of confusion and absurdity, he presents the social framework
of his tales in a tragic and more modern dimension. He sees
in 'the *train dont va* English society before one's eyes—the great
modern collapse of all the forms and "superstitions" and
respects, good and bad, and restraints and mysteries . . .
decadences and vulgarities and confusions and masculinizations
and feminizations—the materializations and abdications and
intrusions, and Americanizations, the lost sense, the brutalized
manner—the publicity, the newspapers, the general revolution,
the failure of fastidiousness'.

The European scenes and the international elite described
are James' own : if at times he magnifies and embellishes their
features—as the environment he knew and loved best—more
frequently his analysis is realistic, lucid, without illusions. He
could be easily considered as the historian—the first in this
field—of a new Cosmopolis, where continents, contrasting settings, national identities merge. As his *Notebooks* show, he was
careful to observe and study reality around him, to find
his inspiration in some direct contact with appreciation of life.
In this ambition, he went so far as to transgress his particular
domain of interest to apply his attention to the more nationally
localized conflicts of his times. In three of his novels—
*The Bostonians* (1885), *The Princess Casamassima* (1886)
and *The Tragic Muse*—he emerges as a true social novelist,
adjusting his techniques to more utilitarian, current preoccupations.

*The Bostonians*, inspired by Daudet's *Evangelist*, is intended
as a caricature of feminism in the United States; in reality, it
generally surveys the spread of ideas and of the puritan obstinate need to 'regenerate the world'. '. . . The subject is very
national, very typical.' James explains : 'I wished to write a
very *American* tale, a tale very characteristic of our social conditions, and I asked myself what was the most salient and
peculiar point in our social life. The answer was : the situation

of women, the decline of the sentiment of sex, the agitation *on* their behalf.'

The plot is set around the beautiful Verena, the passionate orator of the Boston feminists—'a young prophetess' 'of the redemption of women'. She is directed in her prolific, visionary career by her friend, Olive Chancellor, who believes above all else in reform and innovation : 'essentially a celibate', 'a rapacious woman', this lady's excessive and possessive friendship for her is probably not altogether disinterested and pure. So, James describes the struggle for Verena's affections between Olive and Basil, her own cousin, who is also in love with the young prodigy. However, the novel draws its interest and best effects not from this sentimental intrigue, but from the vivid, satirical depiction of the propaganda activities of the two women, their peculiar Boston environment of cheap and naïve intellectual effervescence, replete with eccentrics of every kind, 'spirit—rappers and roaring radicals!' Basil-Ransome wondered who they all were; he had a general idea that they were 'mediums, communists, vegetarians'.

The elderly Miss Birdseye, a secondary character in the novel, is even more typical of this odd assembly : 'The brevity of her simple garment was the one device by which Miss Birdseye managed to suggest that she was a woman of business, that she wished to be free for action. She belonged to the Short-Skirts League, as a matter of course; for she belonged to any and every league that had been founded for any purpose whatever. This did not prevent her being a confused, entangled, inconsequent, discursive old woman, whose charity began at home and ended nowhere, whose credulity kept pace with it, and who knew less about her fellow-creatures, if possible, after fifty years of humanitary zeal, than on the day she had gone into the field to testify against the iniquity of most arrangements. . . . She looked as if she had spent her life on platforms, in audiences, in conventions, in phalansteries, in *seances*; in her faded face there was a kind of reflection of ugly lecture-lamps. . . . She talked continually, in a voice of which the spring seemed broken, like that of an overworked bell-wire. . . .'

In the midst of similar awkward specimens, Verena appears
as 'supremely innocent', misled and exploited, and quite willing to be rescued by Basil. The only one to keep calm in the
general excitement of ideas, he remains unmoved by the 'right
and wrongs of women, the equality of the sexes, the hysterics
of conventions . . .'; he rejects the mad pursuit of hasty, irrelevant, utopian reforms, and summarizes his impressions as follows : '. . . it's a feminine, a nervous, hysterical chattering,
canting age, an age of hollow phrases and false delicacy and
exaggerated solicitudes and coddled sensibilities, which, if we
don't soon look out, will usher in the reign of mediocrity of
the feeblest and flattest and the most pretentious that has ever
been'.

Despite a tendency toward melodrama and a loose structure,
*The Bostonians* is undoubtedly James' best social novel, the
only one containing a broad and truthful description of American realities. The naturalist features are barely evident, but
satire and criticism become almost too sharp and facile. James
attacks the excessive, mediocre idealism that dangerously infects America, the over-zealous crusaders and evangelists of
varied sorts who are set on regenerating humanity at all costs.
The novel thus outranges its subject—feminism and Boston
intellectualism—in order to analyse a very dominant trait of
American life and character.

*The Princess Casamassima* is another Jamesian attempt to
examine the social upheavals of his time. Ambitious, closer to
the method of Zola, James considers class-conflict and revolution. It is about the 'real London, the people and their suffer-
ings and passions'; 'about the lower orders, the rising
democracy, the spread of nihilism, and all that'.

James describes the wretchedness of the slums and the poor
who inhabit them—a little dressmaker, a shopgirl, a plain
workman, a revolutionary from the Paris Commune, and
Hyacinth, the hero, a bookbinder by trade. He is the natural
son of a simple French seamstress and a wealthy English peer—
who had been tragically bound by love and misfortune. In
some unusual circumstances, his mother had killed her lover,

and later had died in prison. Since his childhood Hyacinth has been aware of his unhappy origin and the family crime; he now rails against the conventions, the injustices of the established social order which had prevented his parents from marriage, from living according to their choice. Burdened by the consequences, he sees himself as one of the 'disinherited', and he espouses the cause of the revolution : '. . . there is an immense underworld, peopled with a thousand forms of revolutionary passion and devotion . . .' he proclaims. 'And on top of it all, society lives ! People go and come, and buy and sell, and drink and dance, and make money and love, and seem to know nothing and think of nothing; and iniquities flourish, and the misery of half the world is prated about as a "neccessary evil", and generations rot away and starve in the midst of it, and day follows day and everything is for the best in the best of possible worlds. All that is one half of it, the other half is that everything is doomed ! In silence, in darkness, but under the feet of each one of us, the revolution lives and works. It is a wonderful immeasurable trap, on the lid of which society performs its antics.'

Hyacinth belongs to a revolutionary group; he promises his comrades, when the time is ripe, to commit an act of terrorism. But, soon, he comes under the influence of the Princess Casamassima, an international adventuress who, out of love for danger and novelty, 'wishes to throw herself into the revolution, to guide it, to enlighten it'. Attracted by Hyacinth, before dispersing all her fortune for the good cause, she enables him to experience the life of the rich and the privileged. A short visit to Paris and to Venice makes him 'deeply demoralized'; he understands the benefits 'of civilization as we know it, based if you will upon all the despotisms, the cruelties, the exclusions, the monopolies and the rapacities of the past, but thanks to which, all the same, the world is less impracticable and life more tolerable'. He no longer believes in the 'party of action' —and international movement controlled by clandestine forces and invisible men; he revolts against blind obedience and the suppression of individual thinking. At the end, he does not assassinate a dignitary, as he is ordered; instead he shoots himself.

*The Princess Casamassima* is one of James' most sombre novels. Hyacinth's trials and struggles occur in a foggy and depressing London, a poetic rather than a realistic evocation, dominated by inexorable condemnation. In addition, treachery appears everywhere : he is betrayed by Millicent, the girl he loves; the Princess loses interest in him, takes up with his best friend; and in Muniment, the dedicated party man who represents the revolutionary ideals, he discovers insincerity as well. Hyacinth 'will expect a good deal more of life than he will find in it. That's why he won't be happy.' Indeed—although he is naïvely idealistic and poor in ideas—he eagerly seeks in the revolution an absolute value, a moral justification. Uncompromising, true to himself, to what he sees, he stands higher than the commitments to socialist justice. Finally he remains alone, surrounded by the ugliness of the world and the collapse of his hopes. At the moment of suicide, he is convinced that all is useless and absurd.

James knows little about the world of politics and still less of the class war; his notion of a conspiracy is hazy and his admirable agitators seem indistinct, rapidly drawn with the conventional lines of operetta-style villains and outlaws. Nevertheless, the novel is a significant example of James' ambition to examine more thoroughly the social inequities and resulting conflagrations. It is, in a way, an extraordinarily modern novel : man trapped between irrepressible political conflicts and ideologies, society no longer stable but corrupted within and threatened from the outside : well-being assailed by misery, idealism by terror, civilization by the will for destruction.

James' third *social* document, *The Tragic Muse* (1890), is even less successful in achieving its aims. The theme is not without relevance to present concerns, but James dramatizes it unevenly and treats it more as a conflict of personal interests than of social conditions. He wishes to depict the confrontation between art and politics—two opposite forces that seem always to exclude each other at the expense of the individual's aspirations—whatever the tendency. The aesthete Nash, the actress Miriam, the painter Nick Dormer want to be independent and devote themselves to their vocations, whereas Nick Dormer's family, his rich fiancée, his ambitious cousin Peter, are attracted by worldly power and public recognition.

The action is set in Paris and then in London, against the background of French theatrical life and that of an English electoral campaign. Some characters—Miriam, for instance—are vivid and convincing, whereas others are less so. Nick and Peter hesitate between politics and art, but one would rather believe them indifferent to both—so weak are their reasoning and their reactions. They do not even seriously pursue the pretty Miriam, who is certainly worth the trouble and willing to answer the challenge. Nick finally renounces his seat in Parliament, thus losing a considerable fortune and the chance of a brilliant marriage; he prefers to lead the difficult, tormented life of an artist, looking for happiness solely in the achievements of his talent. Thus, he brings the novel's theme to a conclusion :

'Ah, you cling to the old false measure of success,' he says. 'I must cure you of that. There will be the beauty of having been disinterested and independent; of having taken the world in the free, brave, personal way. . . . Being is doing, and if doing is duty, being is duty. . . . To be what one *may* be, really and efficaciously. . . . To feel it and understand it, to accept it, adopt it, embrace it, that's conduct, that's life. . . . We must recognize our particular form, the instrument that each of us—each of us who carries anything—carries in this being. Mastering this instrument, learning to play it in perfection—that's what I call duty, what I call conduct, what I call success.'

The interest of the book, however, is less in the struggle between art and politics and more in the sombre picture of contemporary family and society, where the young people are forced into pre-ordained comfortable, mediocre lives and must pay with sacrifices for their right to self-affirmation. In the particular case of Nash, James satirizes *fin de siécle* aestheticism, but on the whole he condemns the predominantly superficial or materialistic standards, the devaluation of individual freedom and of creative pursuits.

Toward the end of his career, outgrowing the strictly naturalist treatment of vast social and political problems, James emerges more as a disillusioned, critical witness of the London and cosmopolitan élites. The splendours of high society no longer dazzle him and he notes the increasing decadence of morals, the indiscriminating rush for intrigue and pleasure; 'the condition of the body,' he writes, 'seems to me to be in many ways very much the same rotten and *collapsible* one as that of the French aristocracy before the revolution, minus cleverness and conversation'.

In *A London Life* and *What Masie Knew*, he describes divorce and adultery; in *The Awkward Age*, love and marriage turned into simple drawing-room games; in *The Pupil* and *Mrs Medwin*, unscrupulous social-climbing; in *The Death of the Lion*, intellectual superficiality. Apparently, society appreciates little beyond platitudes and corruption, exploitation and slander; it is a kind of bargaining place where anything can be traded, bought and sold, in the 'extinction of all sense between public and private. It is the highest expression of the note of "familiarity", the sinking of *manners* . . . which the democratization of the world brings with it.'

James sees this society as obsessed by the appetite for money and luxury. Like Balzac, he considers possesions and fortunes to be driving forces in life, he gives them a dominant rôle in his works. This constitutes for the characters a specific, strong attachment to physical, external realities, even though we never see money being earned by effort or speculation, but only already made : in the form of a dowry, an inheritance—a dimension which guarantees the heroes' freedom, and the possibility of assuaging their enthusiasm for life. But, in the process, it can also become—as if a fatal power or course—the obstacle to happiness, the primary cause of their misfortune. They are finally taken advantage of by their less scrupulous, more covetous friends and relatives. With James, money does not lead so much to dissipation or happy gains as to deep moral corruption, debasing some of his characters and bringing them to treachery and crime. He describes an opulent environment of facility and waste, but not without constantly stressing 'the force of the money-power', in this 'world of money': it is the devious instrument to wealth and opportunity in the finest sense, only later to reveal itself possessing its holders. Throughout James' works, it can be seen as the particular symbol of all the material forces with which the individual—in his fight to obtain or renounce fortune—is in perpetual conflict.

James had understood 'the lesson of Balzac' (whom he called 'the father of us all'); he too wanted his work to be a *comédie humaine*—an image of the life of his own time. As his social novels demonstrate, he wished to study the grave upheavals in society, but it can hardly be said that he confronted the real issues. He lacked interest in and knowledge of anything like economics, political sciences, historical evolution, or mere sociological data. On the other hand, with the years, he had lost touch with a specific milieu or country; he found it hard to understand the growing diversified America; as for England and Europe and their domestic problems, he only knew them on the outskirts, as a foreign observer. Even the broader aspects of his works are only evidence of individual destinies and intimate ordeals, of the torments and aspirations of certain select cosmopolitans. Their interest as documents lies in the observation and depiction of this rather remote, restricted class and its inordinate manners and preoccupations; what is more, the approach is strictly psychological, everything is seen through the individual consciousness. Only in this particular domain could James be called a *moral* historian—thus reminding us of Proust rather than Balzac.

With his ambition to leave behind a picture of manners, James seems more like a typical nineteenth-century novelist, although he has less of the nineteenth-century novelist's capacity for a topical and characteristic, external and forceful realism: one does not read James for descriptions of nineteenth-century manners in the usual sense, and he is yet some way from the refracted subconscious realism of the twentieth-century psychological novel.

He was deeply convinced that the writer should touch only indirectly on physical and everyday aspects of existence; he criticizes Balzac for 'his inordinate passion for detail'. After his 'social' novels, his fictional world becomes increasingly closed; his characters rarely venture outside; the action is set by the fireside, in the drawing-room or the nearest garden. If the details still seem abundant and carefully studied, it is because their range is extended by suggestion. And what characterizes more James' portrayal of society is his vision of its disintegrating process : he is impressed less by the permanent, normal, typifying features that generally attract the attention of the realist, than by the cold irrelevance of reality, the inconsistency of human behaviour, the confusion of norms and ideas, the state of simple fusion and evolvement that matters seem to follow—outside any guiding principle, or even orientation. He saw the rapid changes in manners, taste, material well-being in this *fin de siècle* society : he terms it 'the modern madness', 'the universal menagerie', 'the awful modern crust'. He transcribed in his works the 'convulsions' he had observed, by giving them a sense almost of absurdity.

James' view of the intrusive, silent presence of objects and facts is increasingly symbolic—they are mere signs of the external world and only their manifestation within the human consciousness can create actuality and meaning. For the conflict between the individual and society, the preferred topic for most nineteenth-century novelists, James substitutes a conflict of exchanges and connexions on the level of perception and experience : concrete reality, and the way it appears, is gradually identified with a phenomenological revelation, until it becomes a vast sensible amalgam of all the images and suggestions persistently imposed and imprinted by it. The heroes seem to move in a maze of imponderable, fluctuating, deceitful projections, which at any moment change position, withdraw, cast shadows or new significances. Reality with James lies always elsewhere than where one first saw it. Although he is himself unable to explore all the possibilities of this new approach, he already shows future writers the simultaneous contours of the apparent and the hidden, the reassuring and the threatening aspects of significance. In other words, James opens the way to an integral realism with an essentially psychological basis of questioning and wondering : a dimension for which the word 'realism' is no longer an adequate description.

# 5. Oppression and Liberty

IN MOST cases, the Jamesian man stands aloof from his environment. Nevertheless, he is a conscious social being who never rebels against society and the established order; in travelling to foreign lands, he wishes to find a new place in life but not removed from the destiny of others or from the forms and requirements of culture and tradition. He aspires less to escape to complete freedom than to interior fulfilment, which implies involvement, confrontation with the difficulties, complications, embarrassments imposed by all human relations. In his efforts to achieve the life he desires, he is often subjected to family and social oppression—a series of obstacles raised against his will and his rights, demands made unjustly upon him, which he cannot accept without giving up his struggle to live. In his childhood James had suffered from the domination of his family and, as a result, he remained convinced that the family, whether American or European, represents tyranny—a blind force defending its interests and morality, fostering a mediocre closed-in existence, standing between man and his happiness. Most frequently he places his young heroes outside the family setting, their parents gone, rarely having a brother or sister; when living with their families, they are always in a particular moral state—somehow diminished, timid, uncertain of themselves—if not simply suffering and unhappy.

*Washington Square* (1880), a novel recalling the theme of Balzac's *Eugenie Grandet*, is the most searching of James' family dramas. Catherine, the heroine, a girl of twenty, 'was not ugly, she had simply a plain dull, gentle countenance'. 'Though she was an heiress, no one had ever thought of regarding her as a belle'; '. . . she was shy, uncomfortably, painfully shy. . . . In reality, she was the softest creature in the world.'

She has lost her mother and lives in New York with her father—a doctor—and her aunt : a typical bourgeois existence in a large house on Washington Square. She experiences the first intimations of love when courted by Morris; but her father, who thinks Morris merely a 'fortune-hunter', threatens to dis-inherit her if she accepts his advances. However, her aunt, 'a woman of powerful imagination' and starved of intrigue and excitement, motivates her toward the most romantic escapades, clandestine meetings and a secret marriage. Pressed from all sides, tormented and abused, also discovering that Morris' in-terest is possibly not sincere, Catherine endures a moral crisis in which she doubts her own mind and the course of events to come; she neither wishes to disobey her father nor to abandon her fiancé; 'She has an entirely new feeling, which may be described as a state of expectant suspense about her own actions. She watched herself as she would have watched another person, and wondered what she would do. It was as if this other person, who was both herself and not herself, had sud-denly sprung into being, inspiring her with a natural curiosity as to the performance of untasted functions.'

A silent, stubborn struggle commences between Catherine and her father : they face each other like enemies, increasingly unyielding. He does not openly constrain her, wishes 'to leave his daughter her liberty', but at the same time treats her with irony, overwhelms her with his indifference and contempt. This ungentle, if not cold attitude, estranges Catherine from him; she sees herself alone in the presence of disparaging forces beyond her control and relapses into fearful, oppressive torpor : 'Catherine's days, at this time, were dismal, and the weight of some of her hours was almost more than she could bear'. Realizing that her aunt is only amusing herself with her love-affair, that her father does not care to help her and has never loved her, she is also finally abandoned by Morris. All understanding and affection seem denied her and she no longer wants to share her suffering with anyone, particularly with her family : 'You mustn't pity me; I don't mind it now; I am used to it . . . I mind everything less. I feel differently, I feel separated from my father. . . . Then I made up my mind. I will never ask him for anything again, or expect anything from him. It would not be natural now.' Marked by this general rejection, doomed to remain a forlorn spinster, Catherine's personality changes; at the end, she chooses her solitary reclusion and refuses to abandon it. When Morris comes to her years later, she turns him out; as for her father, she treats him now with polite disdain : 'Nothing could ever undo the wrong or cure the pain that Morris had inflicted on her, and nothing could ever make her feel toward her father as she felt in her younger years. There was something dead in her life.'

*Washington Square* is one of the first of James' psychological novels; the tension created is essentially an inner tension, the drama between the characters strictly follows the progression and the gradual slackening of their emotional build up. Catherine's adventure occurs within her mind, in her experience of disillusionment and evil. Her conflict results less from her brief, unfortunate attachment to Morris than from the irresponsive, reckless domination of her family. Her father never realizes that she is young, that being plain and shy, her hopes are not many, that within herself she bears a silent longing for love and life. In opposing her marriage to Morris (who undoubtedly would make her unhappy and squander her fortune)—he does not save, but actually ruins his daughter's future : she misses her only chance for possible happiness and illusion, if not mere involvement in worldly existence. His oppression is entirely moral, contravening as it does Catherine's conscience and emotions. Catherine's ultimate victory, in her refusal of everything and her acceptance of fate, is a victory of dignity and pride; but her own existence will remain on the fringe of others' lives.

In James' works, society is—no less than the family—presented as an enemy of individual freedom. It promotes oppression with its established principles and rules of conduct, its *do's* and *dont's*, which almost never correspond to what is true for each individual. It incarnates, moreover, a number of vices and evils—slander, corruption, greed, indifference; it also germinates a parasitism that feeds on the innocents' youth and fortune. It thwarts the individual's destiny with its judgments on his acts and nature.

⌈As the Jamesian hero's trial is mainly a struggle between what he is and has, and what he wishes to be and obtain, only through experience—human contacts, earthly and worldly gains—can he carry out his goals : society appears, therefore, as the particular sphere of his endeavour and of his inevitable clash with disappointing realities. Surrounded by people who do not understand him, who try to dupe and abuse him, his adventure—more or less doomed to failure—is essentially a widening of the gulf that divides him from the rest of the world. At the mercy of forces that he can not control, caught in a crisis where he only gropes his way, it is ultimately his consciousness that, in the revelations it acquires, is invaded, disturbed, oppressed⌋There, the real confrontation with social evils occurs, and the hero is never really victorious⌉ like Catherine of *Washington Square*, he can only retreat in a dignified isolation, negating the values and joys of the world.

James intensely dramatizes the 'ferocious and sinister' aspect of society and existence. He has a profound sense of the dark, malevolent forces that confront man, that play—somehow amusingly, ironically—in the background of his most positive intentions. One could almost say that James' conception of Evil is somewhat religious, biblical or apocalyptic, so strongly does it carry with it an image of disruption, if not eternal damnation—though only within the realm of the human and the psychological. Evil is not seen so much as a condition—destitution, physical suffering, social injustices, reprehensible acts, but rather as a relentless torture, active both on the subconscious and conscious planes, a violence inflicted upon the self, opposing and tarnishing truth and confidence in the individual.

James places his heroes in extreme situations where personal interests and ambitions are at war, but the real antagonisms never occur in the open; instead, they grow and spread only as reflections and inner reactions. There is less struggle than strain. Many of the unscrupulous schemers that we meet embody—along with their greed for material advantages—a moral greed and possessiveness that feed on and consummate their victims' innocent and idealistic nature. Mme Merle says with cold assuredness in *Portrait of a Lady* : 'I don't pretend to know what people are meant for . . . I only know what I can do with them'.

Faced with such dangers, it is not any more a matter of defending one's liberty, happiness and fortune; it is a matter of the preservation and the survival of man's sovereignty. If James' mischievous characters exist in their inability to respect their equals, there are many who, on the contrary, act with supreme tolerance, with the desire to understand rather than judge, with the moral scruple to refuse their right to justice or revenge when this interferes with the will and freedom of others. They would rather not compromise their own. Once they have guessed at or ever so slightly touched on human pettiness and corruption, they awaken to a new moral sensibility; they choose moral commitment. Now more responsible than before, through their infinitely thoughtful attentions and reflections, they comply not so much to a code of propriety and good form, as to an ethic that makes profound spiritual demands and must guarantee their lasting human quality. Abandoning all conduct founded on selfish motives—and almost happy to act to the detriment of their own interests— their newly oriented intentions and decisions apparently will be recognized, rewarded in some mysterious, unexpected way, sometimes, somewhere, beyond their present predicament : they never see their actions within real time, but as if projected on to the ascending curve of their total experience, the tendency of which is straight-forwardness, integrity and the highest possible condition of the soul. They refuse to compromise with evil; they deny themselves love and friendship, success and wealth, when such rewards must depend on the suffering of others.

*The Spoils of Poynton* (1897) is a short novel, which appears
at first to be a comedy of English manners. The central theme
is Fleda's caution and restraint as against influencing the future
of Owen Gereth, who loves her, although he is engaged to
Mona. Mrs Gereth has 'made sure of Fleda' and prompts her
to marry Owen; she wants—and this is her sole concern—to
prevent the 'barbaric' Mona from becoming mistress of her
house of Poynton (where she stores her collection of valuable
furniture), for Mona intends to 'mod' the establishment. Mrs
Gereth uses Fleda unscrupulously in her plan to save the
precious 'trophies': she is 'one of those who impose, who inter-
fuse, themselves'. Fleda rebels against the possibility of any
'interference' in her relationship with Owen who, though interested in her, is hesitant; she feels a victim of intrigue, nothing
more than a pawn in Mrs Gereth's strategy. According to her,
Owen and Mona should decide their future by themselves,
without outside pressures; she will marry Owen only if Mona
—by her own reason and decision—allows him his freedom:
'If he was in a plight he must get out of the plight himself,'
she says to herself, 'he must get out of it first, and anything he
should have to say to anyone else must be deferred and
detached. She herself at any rate—it was her own case that
emerged—couldn't dream of assisting him save in the sense
of their common honour. She could never be the girl to be
drawn in; she could never lift her finger against Mona. There
was something in her that would make it a shame to her for
ever to have owed her happiness to an interference . . . and
merely to have abstained even wouldn't sufficiently assure her
she had been straight. Nothing was really straight but to justify
her little pensioned presence by her use. . . . Of a different
manner of loving she was herself ready to give an instance,
an instance of which the beauty indeed would not be generally known. . . . Even in the ardour of her meditation, Fleda
remained in sight of the truth that it would be an odd result
of her magnanimity to prevent her friend's shaking off a woman
he disliked.'

Fleda's disinterested, careful attitude helps resolve the Poynton dispute without crises. She overcomes her love for Owen and prefers renunciation to the slim chances of happiness; so the marriage between Owen and Mona finally occurs. She achieves a kind of 'greatness' in her 'generosity'—a satisfaction of her 'moral sense' in not having violated the freedom of her partners in fate.

Fleda has a true sister in the more remarkable Maggie Verver of *The Golden Bowl* (1904), James' last novel and one of his masterpieces.

Daughter of an American millionaire art collector, Maggie marries, in London, an Italian prince, Amerigo. Soon after, her father, a widower, marries Charlotte, an old friend of Maggie's whom she hasn't seen for years. Without the Ververs' knowledge, Charlotte was formerly the prince's mistress; now the two lovers find a favourable opportunity to renew their relationship. Maggie and her father, fond of each other and used to intimacy, often prefer to be alone. When sufficient impressions and incidents accumulate, Maggie perceives the anomaly of the situation, and her struggle to re-establish a proper equilibrium begins.

The four main characters and Mrs Assingham, their confidante, act toward one another with the greatest tact and scrupulousness so that they may never harm one another or destroy their common illusion of happiness. Amerigo and Charlotte can be faulted for their passion and deceitful conduct, but they are not evil or corrupt like other lovers in James' fiction : 'Their situation . . . is too extraordinary. . . . They make it credible. . . . They believe in it themselves. They take it for what it is and that . . . saves them. And the beauty . . . is that they are afraid for them. Afraid, I mean, for the others.' Charlotte, although she feels no remorse, is not oblivious of Maggie's overburdened position; she tells the prince that 'we mustn't take advantage of her character'. Amerigo himself, somewhat tired of his wife, and, morally, less exacting and sensitive than her, wishes however to protect her from needless suffering. He loves her still, and it is enough for her to harbour suspicions and voice doubts, for him to neglect his mistress and try every means to reassure and recover her. But he shows no less consideration for Charlotte when he hides from her Maggie's growing knowledge of their relationship, to spare her from embarrassment with respect to Maggie.

As for Maggie, she seems to be apart, above the situation and passions involved. Her attitude is one of stately forgiveness and sympathy, independent of personal interest, forcefully expressed. Charlotte herself admits that 'she's not selfish enough. There's nothing, absolutely, that one *need* do for her. She is so modest . . . she doesn't miss things. I mean if you love her—or, rather, I should say if she loves you. She lets it go . . . she lets everything go but her own disposition to be kind to you. It's of herself that she asks efforts—so far as she has ever to ask them. She hasn't much. She does everything herself. And that's terrible.' Maggie's drama is that she finds herself faced for the first time with evil—prevarication and adultery, if not incest : Charlotte is not only her personal friend, but also her step-mother. She is bothered, however, less by the idea of immorality than by the inadmissible irony of her condition : she aspires to eliminate ugliness, physical dependency, underhand deeds, and general insincerity from her rarefied, opulent world. When she discovers the secret of her husband's affair with Charlotte, she does not resort to jealousy, explanations, overt conflict : she is particularly eager to safeguard her father's peace and illusions, for he is also deceived by Charlotte—his wife. Her attitude reveals her desire to preserve individual liberty, and find a solution within the consciences of the other three.

As Mrs Assingham says, '. . . the only thing that ever *can* be the matter with Maggie is . . . her beginning to doubt. To doubt, for the first time . . . of her wonderful little judgement, of her wonderful little world. . . . She won't "put" it anywhere. She won't do with it anything anyone else would. She'll take it all herself. . . . She has taken them over. . . . Maggie was the person in the world to whom a wrong thing could least be communicated. It was as if her imagination had been closed to it, her sense altogether sealed. That therefore . . . is what will now *have* to open. Her sense will have to open . . . to what's called

Evil—with a very big E : for the first time in her life. To the
discovery of it, to the knowledge of it, to the crude experience
of it. . . . They'll have had to be disagreeable to make her
decide to live. . . . To live . . . for her father. . . . She'll have
to save *him* . . . to keep her father from her own knowledge.
*That* . . . will be work cut out ! . . . She won't be lost if her
father's saved. She'll see that as salvation enough. . . . Rather
—she's a little heroine.'

Maggie's extraordinary achievement is to assume the full
burden of the situation—hard as it may be. She pretends that
nothing is the matter, that nothing has changed; she only
adopts a new attitude toward the lovers, without hostility or
even intimations, an attitude of insistently kind, almost protective, attention, which makes them understand that she
*knows*. She has them meet in her presence on several occasions;
these intense confrontations create a state of uneasiness, engen-
der a series of doubts in their conscience, bring forward
Maggie's case, Maggie's person, which they have overlooked,
dispensed with in their happy passionate pursuit. The only
real result that she wished to obtain is to persuade her father—
though indirectly, tacitly—to return to America with Charlotte. In restoring order, Maggie does not at any moment conceive of redressing rights as such or of having the lovers *pay*
for their misconduct : she wants to convey the impression that
they have decided by themselves the new course of action and
that, all things considered, nothing unpleasant or irreparable
has occurred. The gradual process of reversal, of new relations,
has been an interplay of the individual consciousness, everyone being free to claim the outcome as his own doing and freely
to resume his life. The crisis between the four protagonists
dispurses because not only Maggie, but all of them share a
'mutual consideration', 'a conscious care . . . of every hour,
literally'. Maggie, however, is the centre—the clearing point,
so to say—where the mysterious exchanges take place; not
they, but she now plays the game, keeping them waiting,
anxious, dependent on her slightest moves of forgiveness and
help: 'It all left her . . . with the strangest of impressions—

the sense, forced upon her as never yet, of an appeal, a positive confidence from the four pairs of eyes, that was deeper than any negation, and that seemed to speak on the part of each of some relation to be contrived by her, a relation with herself, which would spare the individual the danger, the actual present strain, of the relation with the others. They thus tacitly put it upon her to be disposed of, the whole complexity of their peril. . . . She was there, and there just *as* she was, to lift it off them. . . .'

Maggie rejects oppression by avoiding hurt feelings and hasty action, by refusing to judge the lovers for their predicament. Her moral feat is to try to resolve all difficulties entirely by her own judgement and means, thus sparing them guilt or the avowal of their relationship. She is content simply to bring to awareness—but not to overt knowledge—the discordant, unnatural, aspect of their common situation, and to give the first example of responsible and magnanimous conduct, which then provokes a similar reaction. In this way, Maggie rediscovers not only peace and happiness—mere externals—but the satisfaction of having saved her partners and herself from plunging forever into the abyss of possessive emotions and resentment.

James would not be so interested in social and family oppression if he was not so concerned with the freedom of selfhood —a theme which he develops not only as contacts, happenings, conflicts (which he does, finding some of his most dramatic plots), but above all at the crossroads of the individual's place and commitment in existence : a moral stratification, a moral belonging. More is at stake than the victory of good or evil, than the fight between the 'good guys' and the 'bad guys' : the clash of the 'self' with family and society—seen as exploitation and interference—brings out the urgent need for the individual's choice of the quality of his being and the kind of existence (in essence) that he wants to lead : all of him, mind and spirit, is too deeply involved in a given situation, and the situation is never resolved (whatever the actual, practical outcome) unless he *comes out*—walks into the open, so to speak—

and decides with final determination to set on, to be himself.
The freedom implied, therefore, is not to be confused with
freedom of movement and decision (the right to travel, marry,
engage in such or such endeavours, etc.); the freedom emphasized in the presence of oppression is liberty of spirit—an uncon-
trollable personal dimension answerable only to the conscious
self and its highest purpose, whose tenets escape any social rule
or human authority.

The Jamesian heroes' presence in the world does not only
appear as a social conflict on the plane of reality, but on a more
abstract plane, as a conflict with evil and fate. They are less
eager to search for earthly happiness than for the conviction
to that they have found and fulfilled their destiny. This places
them in a tragic situation, in a tragic rôle, for they apprehend
an inevitable condemnation—burdened with, chained as they
are to conditions, to people, to oppression; only by enduring a
catharsis, admitting the chance of possible personal destruction
and the danger of failure, can they discover their way out—
heroically, as it were: but this is, of course, never success in
the ordinary, worldly sense. As their efforts consist in establish-
ing a closer relationship between environment and consciousness, and as the result is more of a divergence than a cohesion,
they logically exist in a state of crisis and tension; they cannot
resolve through external arrangements, through compromises
with circumstances, their strictly inner conflict and quest:
similar to the French classical heroes, they can only act in the
direction of solitary splendour and the acceptance of fate. They
seem heroic, for being the sole arbiters of their choice, all their
actions—magnified in the process—acquire a culminating, irre-
vocable importance: fully responsible and aware, they carry
alone the weight, the strain of their predicament.

Always moving between the narrow lines of failure and success, at the same time compelled to act, and restrained in their
action by their scruples, the heroes do not conceive their examples and experiences as exclusively their own; they see
them as a possible reaffirmation of general human values. They
face the others in their adventure not only dramatically and

pragmatically, but with the idea that the degree of existence which they choose and define—together—will have its full content only if no one has been hurt or ignored: they have to protect and preserve everyone's freedom, not theirs alone, and if they succeed, they consider this to be sufficient justification. They refuse, therefore, to damage the rights of others; they abandon complacency and interests, and prefer the harder road of mutual generosity and respect of selfhood. 'Richly responsible' and 'just' in the 'great conscience they possess', they adopt the simple greatness of sacrifice and renunciation.

The best of them exist 'in the cold upper air of finer discrimination', seeking for 'the most exquisite conceivable' in their contacts and attachments, unceasingly analysing the import of their words and their actions, 'cultivating thanklessly the considerate and the delicate'. Although they grasp their own right to independence, they are never negligent, brusque or exacting: 'There are things sacred—whether they're joys or pains. But one can always, for safety, be kind . . . one feels when that's right.' Everyone seems to delineate his sphere of obligation and suffering with a stronger sense of pride: 'Whatever happens to me,' says one hero, 'let me not be unjust . . . let me bear my burdens myself, not shift them upon others.' . . . 'It's always a question of doing the best for one's self one can —without injuring the others.' They all seek contentment and glory beyond oppression, beyond the personal, in the greater moral beauty of their greater moral consciousness. One critic has concluded that 'the moral sense is for them a kind of chivalry'.

'. . . You are noble,' James wrote to Grace Norton, 'when your interest and pity as to everything that surrounds you, appear to have a sustaining and harmonizing power. Only don't, I beseech you, *generalize* too much in these sympathies and tenderness—remember that every life is a special problem which is not your's but another's, and content yourself with the terrible algebra of your own. Don't melt too much into the universe, but be as solid and intense and fixed as you can. We all live together, and those of us who love and know, live the most. We help each other—even unconsciously, each in our own effort, we lighten the effort of others, we contribute to the sum of success, make it possible for others to live.'

# 6. *Enthusiasm for Life*

CHARLES DU BOS wrote that 'Henry James' ultimate aim is, as it were, to retrieve as much as possible of life by an act of transfiguration—by enclosing it for ever in the work of art'. And according to the novelist himself, he always attempts to express, through his particularly chosen plots and themes, 'the multitudinous presence of all human situations and pictures, the surge and pressure of *life*'.—

If such statements apply more to the revelatory technique of James than to any philosophical intention, they point out, none the less, his constant preoccupation with life—seen not only as a process of experience and development, but as a living and culminating force, as a confrontation with meaningful stresses, as a search for explanation and significance in each individual's destiny. Most of the main characters are endowed with an exceptional enthusiasm for life : they 'want to live', to 'get everything out of life'; they 'adopt life' and they 'cling to life'. In their urge for romance and liberation, in their desire for human contacts or aesthetic pleasure, the final purpose of their choice is to gain a deeper, more intimate knowledge of their involvement : 'Ah, aren't we very much the same—simple lovers of life ? That is, of that finer essence of it which appeals to the consciousness.' Their enthusiasm is displayed in feverish impatience to 'see', 'feel', 'know', 'understand' the world and people. Comparable to explorers eager to penetrate new lands and cultures, to open to themselves new fields of challenge and discovery, there is a strictly 'empirical' side of their nature— as James calls it—'empirical' not only because it is experimental, but also because it is more intellectual than positive,

more of a speculation in the mind than an adherence to
existence. As reflective and introspective beings above all, 'hide-
ously intelligent' and capable of an infinite number of 'refinements . . . of consciousness, of sensation, of appreciation', they
expect a primarily moral gratification, something more exacting than the mere emotions and impressions intensely acquired
—to which they never completely submit. Life is offered to
them as a free choice, not a contingency. Therefore they can
aspire to a more positive sense of living and to richer personal
trials. Isabel Archer (heroine of *The Portrait of a Lady*) is
typical of all of them when she says, 'I am very fond of my
liberty', and when she defends her right to choose in the world
whatever she wishes, even to 'choose some atrocity'. Because
of their material security or general absence of career and
family obligations, their first move is to set on, to travel, to go
elsewhere, (as a greater liberation), and then to seek a stronger
affirmation, a wider responsibility for themselves: 'One must
be what one is' . . . 'We have to judge for ourselves. . . . We
see our lives from our own point of view; that is the privilege
of the weakest and the humblest of us.' In short, they neglect
interests and pleasures as such, that lead to restriction and submission; they all share a marked 'prejudice in favour of the
free exploitation of life', to attain fearless human pride in face
of destiny, i.e. 'to look at life for oneself'.

Most frequently, James attributes such tendencies to his
American heroes: the Americans, because of their new psychology, their lack of traditions, the fluctuating state of their culture and society, and above all, because of their opportunistic,
enterprising spirit, can best portray personal individualism and
liberty. Moreover, James chooses those Americans ill-adjusted
to their environment, for whom the world of business, material
growth and politics is non-existent. Dissatisfied and frustrated,
languishing in their country, they obscuredly know that their
American surroundings cannot offer them the conflicts, the
greater activity and participation to which they aspire; that
only in escaping, in transcending their condition, can they
achieve lives more intense, and pay—what James calls—their

'tribute to the ideal'. Hence their geographical exile to Europe. As for their moral exile, it results from the sense that belonging, immersion in external, everyday existence, is denied to them both in Europe and in America. Therefore they remain more or less nowhere in relation to commitment, unable to see themselves in the rôle of, say, father, husband, professional man, leader, public personality, or any other rôle that implies an obligation *to* reality. Sensitive and solitary, attracted by intellectual and artistic values, they conceive of life as daring and adventurous only in the realm of inner strivings and tensions; there they look for assurance and success. Because of these particular conditions—which concern general degrees of inevitable personal inadequacy (none the less quite far removed from *angoisse*)—they are precipitated, compelled to face existence.

Jamesian heroes wish to be 'as happy as possible', but this happiness is never achieved without discrimination on their part. They possess an instinctive fear of cruelty and ugliness, of unappealing insubordinate, improper manifestations, if not of simple physical conduct as sensuality or boldness: they are always attracted by order and harmony, by meticulously studied gestures and graceful attitudes of politeness. Morality, however, never dictates such preferences, but a highly developed sense for Style, Form, perfection, and an almost classical sense of purity and poise. They all would like to see their lives as miraculous, faultless works of art: for them 'taste [plays] a considerable part in emotions' and they earnestly aspire to 'moral beauty'. If sometimes one is tempted to compare them to the aesthetes of the turn of the century—those whose personalities seem today exceedingly outdated and artificial—one sees them nevertheless in this extreme delineation or narrow margin of existence, not as vegetating in sophistications. Rather, they are dominated by a sincere, forceful desire, almost a necessity for their nature, not to accept easy, more or less vulgar satisfaction in the world; but to seek out instead —and be conscious of it at any moment—only a small number of privileged hours, of crowded happenings, which will give them the sudden though ephemeral sense of having lived. Never abandoning themselves to action, never submerged by emotions or carried away by ambition, their enthusiasm for life becomes a primary adventure of the spirit : the passionate fervour for life is replaced by the knowledge—somehow indirect, incomplete, ambiguous—of having intensely *fèlt* life. The resulting essence of their experience is therefore psychological : locked within themselves, for better or for worse, their incapacity for self-projection, for transcending the self and 'adopting' life, accounts ultimately for their tormented, questioning minds, for their richly endowed—although, so to say, purified and 'saved' from the world—personalities.

Because participation in life finds its achievement on this inner level of exacting moral pursuits—comparable to a degree to the paramount self-respect, *la gloire de soi* of the French Classical Theatre—Jamesian characters conceive their existence, their tragedy, and stake their search for justification and meaning on the plane of heroism and self-denial. In fact, living as they do on the outskirts of immediate experience, although they have ardently asked for it, they have the power of outgrowing it and of remaining unshaken by misfortune : they even '. . . wish that they might find themselves some day in a difficult position, so that they should have the pleasure of being as heroic as the occasion demanded'. Not what happens but why it happens, matters to them, and their unforeseen goal seems always to out-range the very goal that have decided, at first, to attain : they know that 'idealists, in the long run . . . don't *feel* that they lose'. Whatever the case, in choosing Europe and freedom, experiencing life and fully knowing their limitations, they seek to measure themselves against fate, against evil, to triumph again and still be—as they have been in love, travels, introspection and contacts—'great', 'prodigious', 'magnificent', 'sublime'.

The young heroines of James', aspiring to 'one crowded hour of glorious life', are the best expressions of this enthusiasm—not so much more like Daisy Miller, imprisoned in their conduct and unaware of their ordeal, but those like Isabel Archer and

Milly Theale, who acquire new consciousness and possess stronger capacity for enduring the strains of human conflict. They constitute a finer image—an idealization almost—of James' cousin, Minny Temple, whom he loved and admired and whom he calls 'a plant of pure American growth', 'the heroine of our common scene'. She died young, without being able to satisfy her impatience and fervour for life. Her portrait, as drawn by James, explains more than one aspect of the unusual personalities of his protagonists: 'She had beyond any equally young creature I have known,' he writes, 'a sense for variety of character and play of life in others, for their acting out of their force, of their weakness, whatever either might be, at no matter what cost to herself; and it was this instinct that made her care so for life in general, just as if it was her being thereby so engaged in that tangle that made her, as I have expressed it, ever the heroine of the scene. Life claimed her and used her and beset her—made her range in her groping, her naturally immature and unlighted way from end to end of the scale. . . . She was absolutely afraid of nothing she might come to by living with enough sincerity and enough wonder. . . .'

This description will fit no less precisely Isabel of the *Portrait of a Lady* (1881): young and curious as Minny Temple, eager to free herself from ignorance about life and confront at her own risk the chances of happiness. An orphan child, aimlessly spending her days in the huge, empty family house of Albany, N.Y., she senses a void in her existence—the more or less colourless environment and uneventful future that faces her; she longs for escape, for change, for 'a desire to leave the past behind her and . . . to begin afresh': '. . . it was not with a desire for dozing forgetfulness. It was on the contrary because she felt too wide-eyed and wished to check the sense of seeing too many things at once. Her imagination was by habit ridiculously active. . . . She had a great desire for knowledge, but she really preferred almost any source of information to the printed page; she had an immense curiosity about life and was constantly staring and wondering. She carried within herself a great fund of life, and her deepest enjoyment was to feel the continuity between the movements of her own soul and the agitations of the world.'

Prompted by such ideas and intuitive possibilities, she decides to visit her aunt, Mrs Touchett, in England; there she immediately understands 'that the note of change had been struck' for her. She shares the opulent existence of the millionaire Touchetts and comes to know English high society—elegant receptions, enormous country places, and general splendour—an existence personified in Lord Warburton, who falls in love with her and would like to marry her. Unexpectedly rich by the death of her uncle, she goes from conquest to conquest: in England, Paris, Florence—wherever her new relationships and countless impressions provide her with the wider, dense experience she has sought. Her story relates the attention she receives from several men, all worthy suitors, all offering her brilliant chances of happiness, but she is not interested in happiness as such: this notion coincides in her mind with a sense of restrictive security, which will hinder the free play of her imagination and her sensations. She wants only to taste life: 'You want to see life. . . . You want to drain the cup of experience' says her cousin Ralph Touchett. 'You've told me the great things that the world interests you and that you want to throw yourself in it.'

Indeed, Isabel, having refused to marry Lord Warburton and Goodwood (a fellow-American also passionately in love with her), because she does not want a happy existence obtained too quickly and without effort, dreams of her complete independence of action and thought, of her right to owe her achievements to no one but herself. 'A rank egoist', she excludes all that may stand between her independent spirit and the desire to dominate alone; as on the other hand, 'too young, too impatient to live, too unacquainted, with pain', she seems mysteriously drawn to some painful, personal ordeal, to a tormented knowledge of 'the misery of the world': 'She always returned to her theory that a young woman whom after all everyone thought clever should begin by getting a general impression of life. This impression was necessary to prevent mistakes, and after it should be secured she might make the unfortunate condition of others a subject of special attention.'

Isabel soon finds herself concerned in the 'unfortunate condition', and more dependent and involved than she ever expected. She marries Osmond: an American expatriated in Italy for many years and by now an inveterate, sophisticated and cold dandy who assumes European prejudices and proprieties literally, but is a man of the arts, a fine conversationalist, and the epitome of elegance and grand style. She had hoped to find with him a life composed of beauty and the finer human qualities, a life replete with fresh, exhilarating impressions; in place of that dream—too innocently conceived—she finds herself 'ground in the very mill of the conventional'. She learns indeed that her dear friend, Mme Merle, who had introduced her to Osmond, was years ago his mistress and that Osmond's delightful daughter, Pansy, is one of the results of this affair (and not of a previous marriage, as was thought). The truth is that Mme Merle has made Osmond marry Isabel solely on account of the latter's considerable fortune, so that they can profit by it and provide Pansy with an exceptional future, a brilliant match. Isabel knows now that Osmond has never loved her; eventually, he stops playing his false, gentle rôle and becomes her tormentor; he pours contempt upon her and denies her freedom. In the presence of suffering, Isabel's experience deepens, acquires a more pronounced personal significance; she chooses not to renounce it, and as she once refused easy happiness, now refuses to be constrained by the denial of happiness. She still sees some use for herself in submitting to her fate but adopting a higher form of sacrifice: she decides to stay for Pansy's sake, to protect her youth and innocence, and rescue her from the dark scheme of Osmond and Mme Merle.

In this manner, Isabel converts her apparent failure of happiness into an awakened, responsive, lucid consciousness of the oppressive evil realities and of her own rôle. She has confronted the complex and often hideous countenance of the world, with-

out having cheated for her own sake or tried to avoid the
dangers and fears that have gradually overtaken her. She had
willed for herself a totality of experience—whatever the price,
even personal destruction—but now, understanding how cun-
ningly she has been exploited by Osmond and Mme Merle,
she masters them with her moral grandeur and does not wish
to change her fully responsible and free state; she is again ready
to face shocks, risks and unknown trials. Nothing can shake
her determination to live to the full extent of her possibilities,
in her dead-locked, hopeless condition; at the end of the novel,
James leaves us with the impression that she will live—in spite
of misfortune—and that her stoic resignation, if not heroic
stand, will have lasting significance for her.

*The Wings of the Dove* (1902) presents a more touching and
dramatic elaboration of enthusiasm for life : 'The idea, reduced
to its essence, is that of a young person conscious of a great
capacity for life, but early stricken and doomed, condemned
to die under short respite, while also enamoured of the world;
aware moreover of the condemnation and passionately desir-
ing to "put in" before extinction as many of the finer vibrations as possible and so achieve, however briefly and brokenly,
the sense of having lived'.

Milly Theale, heiress to a vast fortune and the only survivor
of a once large family, comes to England and to Italy shortly
before her death. She is an unassuming and pale beauty, but
endowed with a peculiar inner resistance and an overpowering
desire for life; like Isabel, she possesses 'a strong and special
implication of liberty, liberty of actions, of choice, of appreciation, of contact'; with a tense, earnest curiosity and
fixity of purpose 'she had come forth to see the world'. Indeed,
in her advantageous situation of unlimited means and opportunities, the future seems to loom bright before her—'the
world's before her'—but from the start she knows herself to
be doomed 'to live fast', to experience a multiude of things
within a short space of time. She would not settle, however, for
tumultuous, hasty, more or less uncouth satisfactions : 'It
wouldn't be for her a question of a flying leap and thereby of a

quick escape. It would be a question of taking full in the face the whole assault of life.'

Europe has for her a message of grandeur, of refined initiations, of new emotions. In London she enters the brilliant circle of Mrs Lowder, and, through her relationship with Lord Mark (who asks her to marry him), her unspoken love for Densher and her friendship with Kate Croy, she succeeds in satisfying—temporarily—'her plea for people and her love for life.' Milly gradually becomes Kate's rival, despite her considerate, gentle attitude toward everyone : in fact, Kate, Mrs Lowder's niece, is promised to Lord Mark, whom she does not love, and secretly is engaged to Densher; therefore both men play the same rôle in her life as in Milly's. Coming from a poor and disgraced family, Kate is anxious to acquire quickly fortune, social status, happiness, and involves Densher in her ambitions. She also has a 'direct talent for life', without the nice conscience of her American friend. When she discovers, unexpectedly, the secret of Milly's approaching death and her desperate love for Densher, Kate hides even more carefully her attachment and engagement to Densher; she now wants him to marry Milly so that—Milly dead—he may become rich, independent, and offer her in turn the freedom and happiness to which she aspires.

In the second half of the novel, the group of English friends has followed Milly to Venice where, ailing most of the time, she lives by herself in an enormous palace. Kate's plan seems to progress : different points of new and various interventions tend to precipitate Densher's marriage to Milly. Mrs Lowder wants to remove him from Kate; others see him as the American girl's last chance of a real life. Densher, a young journalist, as poor as Kate, is at first prepared to share in the plot, for he also wishes 'somehow [to] arrange to annex and possess' life; but when things come to a head he wakes up and rebels against his own moral pliability. Milly, in the meantime, comes closer to the realization that all escape from her fate is impossible. Her doctor had advised her once : 'You've the right to be happy. You must make up your mind to it. You must accept

any form in which happiness may come.' Now, she begins to
live by 'systematic bravado', because she *wants* to live; refusing to be sick, to be pitied, pretending to a perfect calm and
assuredness, she checks her doomed state and hopes that Densher's love will indeed save her. But she gradually feels surrounded by unknown 'abysses', by dark unsuspected revelations,
and Lord Mark, on his part, unfeelingly tells her of Kate's
clever schemes. Milly then understands that Densher has
never been sincere, has never loved her; her enthusiasm
subsides and she lets herself die, deserted, disillusioned, alone in
her empty palace : 'She has turned her face to the wall . . .'
says her friend Suzanne to Densher. 'She doesn't speak at
all. . . . Of nothing—of no one. . . . She doesn't *want* to die.
Think of her age. Think of her goodness. Think of her beauty.
Think of all she is. Think of all she *has*. She lies there stiffen-
ing herself and clinging to it. . . . She's more than quiet. She's
grim. It's what she has never been. So you see—all these days.
I can't tell you but it's better so. It would kill me if she were
to tell me. . . . She'll never tell. . . . She *is* magnificent.' Milly's
last days constitute a purifying, glorifying, if not resurrecting
process—she 'must die . . . in her own extraordinary way' :
'Since I've lived all these years as if I were dead,' she has said,
'I shall die, no doubt, as if I were alive'.

She forgos all that she has pined for and hoped to achieve—
for herself. Her heroism of self-denial unto death brings her to
assert only a higher form of gratification—in generosity, forgiveness and sacrifice. She respects in Kate and Densher the
happiness that she has been denied and, to guarantee their
union beyond risk, she leaves Densher her immense fortune.
She loves him still. Her gesture is to repay him for all his past
kindness and attention, and to give her friend Kate the chance
that she herself has missed. Densher, realizing too late his unworthy, double-faced attitude toward Milly—even though it
has not been entirely his fault—looks for his own redemption
by rejecting the fortune and success at which Kate is so over-
joyed. He refuses to marry her unless they give up the inherited money; he has fallen in love with the memory of the

dove whose wings, in their symbolic leap toward death, have outstretched for a new flight and now cover him. And so Milly is victorious, at last, receiving the love that she could not obtain whilst alive.

The *Wings of the Dove* is one of James' particularly powerful novels, and expresses his desire to give existence a moral significance. Milly's hours of suffering must be converted into hours of affirmation and lasting glory. Like Isabel Archer, she finds fulfilment independently of any search for happiness. Both heroines share the same congenial strife and face similar dangers of being abused and destroyed. The two couples, Osmond-Mme Merle and Kate-Densher, seem equally mischievous, plotting in the background the advantage they can take of their respective, innocent prey. However, Kate and Densher are more subtly drawn, are far less unscrupulous; they can feel real sympathy for Milly—bad because of circumstances, a precipitation of events, rather than by nature. To a degree, they are concerned with Milly's well-being, for in marrying Densher, would she not find the illusion of having known something of love? Her own generosity becomes magnanimity because it is disinterested, given without benefit in return. More than Isabel, she appears throughout the novel as the constant and unchangeable symbol of her own fervour. Whereas Isabel's story ends in a provisional, stoic arrest that presupposes almost no future, Milly's victory is an absolute permanence—a kind of transcendental memory beyond death.

This ultimate awakening to life is also the basic experience of Strether, in *The Ambassadors*. He too '. . . can't, at such a time of day, begin to live . . . yet there stirs in him a dumb passion of desire, of rebellion, of God knows what, in respect to his still snatching a little super-sensual hour, a kind of vicarious joy. . . .' Conscious of his age and his mediocre past, Strether, like Milly, is impatient to explore the new possibilities that chance lays in front of him, to explore them with an extraordinarily alert and attentive consciousness. He has a 'sense of freedom and of a now strongly full initiation'. The path he follows is a tortuous one; he cannot satisfy his desires directly, but only in waiting and wondering, in slowly discovering and too late surrendering himself. But, from the start, he knows 'that there was a precipitation in his fate': his rich impressions of Paris, Chad's youth and affairs, his own latent love for Mme de Vionnet, so many other finer perceptions and relations, convince him—though too late and quite unsuitably for him—of life's highest good, which is to live intensely, as an individually responsible being. Nothing will come of his positive actions: his relationship with Chad's mother, Mme de Vionnet or Miss Gostrey will never bear fruit; his sacrifices will hardly contribute to Chad's future happiness with Mme de Vionnet; he is left to return alone to America, where no one and no life await him. His ordeal would seem to have been entirely useless, had it not, like Milly's, become too inordinate for, too disproportionate to his expectations; by yielding to it finally—seeing his mission in a new light, then the failure of his mission in a still newer light—he achieves, through his very disappointment, personal integrity and greater knowledge of life. His theory about youth, enthusiasm, gratification is only the verbal sublimation of his lost experience. He says to Bilham, a young American painter studying in Paris: '. . . don't forget that you're young—blessedly young; be glad of it, on the contrary, and live up to it. Live all you can; it's a mistake not to. It doesn't so much matter what you do in particular, so long as you have your life. It you haven't had that, what *have* you had? . . . I see it now. I haven't done so enough before—and now I'm old; too old at any rate for what I see. Oh, I *do* see at least; and more than you'd believe or I can express. It's too late. . . . But that doesn't affect the point that the right time is now yours. . . . Don't at any rate, miss things out of stupidity. . . . Do what you like so long as you don't make *my* mistake. For it was a mistake. Live!'

From a particular point of view, the encounter with life, the awakening that results, are not so much conceived as drama of personal involvement or outright external clashes, but as indirect snatches or keen observations (one is affected by what others did or said or missed)—and, therefore, as means of access to some extension of consciousness, after an exposure to evil and emotions unrecognized, in a new and complex world. This attitude is typical of several child-protagonists (*The Pupil*, 1891; *What Masie Knew*, 1897) who achieve a precociously lucid understanding of life around them (their parents' intrigues), but no less of Jamesian heroes in general who—like the author himself—seem always to look at the world from a safe distance, from the wrong end of a telescope, as it were.

James' characters succeed in satisfying their desire to live, but not by tackling an objective of any kind nor an attachment to a public cause. Uprooted and idle, they do not belong anywhere; they remain on the periphery of everyday reality. Even in love and amusement their excessive perceptive powers condemn them in advance to enjoyment without satisfaction. They have no aim other than to discover their own nature, through their own effort. Their experiences appear somewhat gratuitous: action is denied them and they know above all how to explore sensibility. They are conscious of a wasted life, of some goal impossible to reach; their longing for lived fervour, despite the pressing needs and the sincere intensity, never exceeds personal emotion.

Nevertheless, this basic condition is not a restrictive one. For Jamesian characters it is not a question of satisfying certain appetites but of displaying their possession of a constant inner vitality; they are fully aware of *being alive*, of living to the largest extent of their capabilities. Each aspires to accept and show himself as he is, to be worthy of his freedom and to respond to the imperative, higher demands of his own spirit. He wishes to realize his destiny by extending his confrontation with it in a moral sense.

The essential adventure of the Jamesian heroes—whatever they may be—entails a process of becoming, an evolution which proceeds rather abstractly between equally probable and relative dimensions. What they call experience is travelling, visiting the sights and art galleries of Europe, meeting the more or less unwisely selected representatives of a wealthy, worldly, international society; it implies being exposed to intrigues,

whose malevolent import they realize too late, and adjusting
their attitude to that of others; always on the defensive, victi-
mized by and dependent on circumstances, they are never sure
that they have made the right choice and effectively carried out
their plans. For them, success lies in a hypothetical future, beyond their present predicament, in a sublimation of it. Among
themselves, they communicate by means of indistinct gestures
and phrases; reserve and omissions replace direct expression.
This chronic inability to be openly and forcefully *in* the world,
this shying away from all real commitments, explains their
*otherness*, their estranged condition in existence as such, or in
other people's existence. Above all it accounts for their fervent
desire to live, which is the counterpart of (and originates in)
a general, vague sense of inadequacy and frustration. Their
withdrawn attitudes, considerate approaches, furtive appearances, discrete advances, joined with their adventurous Americanism, make them into anachronistic explorers who are turned
inward and whose real fad is to store and direct within themselves a number of impressions and feelings. Their psychology
has something in common with that of cripples who *observe*
life, able to take part in it only indirectly and imperfectly, but
making up for this with excessive interest and eagerness to
know. In their more or less morbid reclusion, they examine
with an almost arbitrary care any phenomenon, any observation, accepting only those enriched by the very strain they are
exerting while reflecting and analysing them. They eventually
see and imagine much more than the facts contain or can
validly suggest. No other course is open to them. They have an
inexhaustible capacity for inner speculation. This continual
mental feverishness becomes the driving force which leads them
forward—though somewhat recklessly and blindly, despite all
their discernment—distorting to a degree their approach to
life and setting them on the periphery of actual involvement.
This therefore compels them even further to rely and dwell
more avidly on their sole and approximate achievements, as
they voluntarily amplify and dramatize them as the centre of
all their preoccupations. True, they want happiness without

rift; they want to meet people, societies, countries; to seize at any cost a permanent, fervent understanding of what it means to suffer and to love: 'Go everywhere . . . do everything, get everything out of life; be happy, be triumphant'. But this is only a war-cry, with a note of exasperation, for a purely experimental programme that they hardly carry out. They behave as cosmopolitan aesthetes, salon intellectuals, actually intimidated by life and other people, imprisoned within their social class, education and past they are guided by their tumultuous imagination and a too scrupulous conscience. Basically, the life they desire to lead, they dare not live, as if it were situated beyond what is permissible and feasible. Their crowding of events and adventures consists in nothing more than to evaluate and justify the least undertaking, to analyse motives and consequences. In this way, by their tireless reasoning they themselves erect, with every moment, mental obstacles which separate them ultimately from what they wish for most; freedom and experience—to burst into the world and lose themselves in action. They ignore spontaneity; they only undergo the inward projection of their desires, which remain suspended in a void, enlivened by an even stronger (though still self-centred) desire 'to live'. Never becoming a fully-realized act, the inner fullness or intensity which is their sole gain—their intimate, intuitive and idealized participation in common human existence—does not liberate them, since it never goes beyond the single consciousness. It is only a transposition of the inability to act into the ability to feel completely; but it excludes both affirmation in the world and absolute transcendence: the enthusiasm for life does not suppose, therefore, an unlimited development, any more than it is the assuagement of earthly aspirations. Only from the moment that the self is restricted, abolished, would it be possible to know perfect freedom and the regenerating results of experience: but with James, although the human consciousness is the most distant, far reaching frontier of his mythical moral world, it is also its limit. The hero remains attached to his conception of himself and of his destiny; he is not able to exceed it. He paces out a closed circle, for even his most daring ventures keep him within the scruples of his own mind, so that in different ways (by constantly speculating and converting) he relives the same mirage, the same disillusionment. At any moment, he is the author of his own fiction and cannot escape self-knowledge. The only delight of this tragic adventure is that, whereas man should remain true to what he happens to be—to the very inadequate resources encompassed by his experience—he should have the courage to go as far as he can in his ambitions and his fervour in order to obtain the maximum expansion of his awakened, extremely acute understanding and his independent, responsible presence.

James' own advice is to 'let your soul live—it's the only life that isn't, on the whole a sell'. 'The great thing is to be *saturated* with something—that is, in one way or another, with life.' He also writes: 'I don't know *why* we live—the gift of life comes to us from I don't know what source or for what purpose; but I believe . . . life is the most valuable thing we know anything about; and it is therefore presumptively a great mistake to surrender it while there is any left in the cup. In other words consciousness is an illimitable power, and though at times it may seem to be all consciousness of misery, yet in the way it propagates itself from wave to wave, so that we never cease to feel, and though at moments we appear to, try to, pray to, there is something that holds one in one's place, makes it a standpoint in the universe which it is probably good not to forsake.'

# 7. *Love without Passion*

EVEN THOUGH love constitutes the basis of most of Henry James' plots, it never appears as a dominant, overwhelming passion. Edmund Wilson writes, with some irritation, that '. . . you cannot enchant an audience with stories about men wooing women in which the parties either never get together or are never seen functioning as lovers'. It would seem, in fact, that Jamesian love is a rather controlled, carefully thought emotion which one is capable of accepting or refusing, according to other, more imperative demands. The lovers are never directly presented as immersed in their involvement; as a rule—in their fierce independence—they never are willing to surrender themselves, to be enslaved by this or any one passion. Their love appears as a tendency or a desire, as a condition of or related to other feelings; and they are never too anxious about the success or the consummation of the affair, somehow afraid or doubtful of its realization. Thinking about the lovers in a projected work, James writes: '. . . they have agreed to give each other up! . . . That is the note on which this particular story would close. This arrangement would be congenial to the characteristic manner of H.J.' [*sic*].

There are rarely examples of love experienced, with its doubts, tribulations and joys: love exists as a probability of the future, as a state of falling in love and wondering about it. James' heroes are more fascinated with the process of eventual achievement than with an actual outcome—again, the experimental pursuit occurs within the individual consciousness rather than on the level of exchange and communication. Furthermore, James prefers to write about love that is latent, barely declared, or has slim chances for success—like Ralph's affection for Isabel, Milly's for Densher, Strether's for Mme de Mionnet. The lovers always seem obscurely convinced of an inevitable impossibility, separation or denial in love; they almost take pleasure—find a kind of glory—when they love in vain. Incapable of yielding to outright expression, or accepting their natural feelings, their love is a dream-like escapade, and it strikes the critic as gratuitous unless by conversion, it assumes another direction and becomes magnanimity or generosity; in such cases, it is another sort of love—human love.

According to James, love also contradicts freedom because it implies possession—the exclusive power of one partner over the other—physical as well as moral possession. He mistrusts marriage and any kind of intimacy where the closeness of the relationship seems to be eventually destructive. 'Whenever two persons are so much mixed up,' says one character, 'one of them always gets more out of it than the other'; '. . . a consuming passion . . . the gratification of it would interfere fatally with the ambition of each of us.'

In *The Portrait of a Lady*, one of James' novels most concerned with love, Isabel Archer is the object of the undeclared though sincere love of her cousin Ralph Touchett. He is the only one to fully understand her, and his lot will be to witness Isabel's unfortunate involvement with other men. Insistently courted by Lord Warburton, passionately loved by Goodwood, who both can offer her security and happiness, she is more attracted by the dilettante aesthete Osmond and his cultivated, diversified existence. Actually, surrounded by so many adventurous opportunities, Isabel is far from falling in love with anyone and hastily making a choice. Typical of many Jamesian heroines, she has an almost pedantic, fastidious approach to love and marriage. A 'cold, hard, priggish person', she looks at her romantic entanglement from the outside and finds that she is 'not too troubled to think'. She is astonished that her suitors are not capable—as she is—of 'making a calculated effort'.

As for marriage, it it is not an abstraction of her mind—in the ignorance of what it requires and entails—it is a sort of bothersome ordeal which a well-bred young person should consider with utmost care. Isabel avoids unpleasant thoughts on '. . . the subject of marriage. The first on the list was a conviction of the vulgarity of thinking too much of it. From lapsing into eagerness on this point she earnestly prayed she might be delivered; she held that a woman ought to be able to live to herself, in the absence of exceptional flimsiness, and that it was perfectly possible to be happy without the society of a more or less coarse-minded person of another sex. . . .' Moreover, Isabel is convinced that marriage offers a too quickly gained—without effort—sheltered and peaceful existence, which hinders the individual's striving for a wider, eventful exploration of the world. She herself does not want to be spared the surprises, the shocks of experience: '. . . I can't escape my fate . . .' she says to Lord Warburton, 'I should try to escape it if I were to marry you. . . . Because . . . I know it is not . . . my fate to give up . . . other chances . . . I don't mean chances to marry. . . . But it comes over me every now and then that I can never be happy in any extraordinary way; not by turning away, by separating myself . . . from life. For the usual chances and dangers, from what most people know and suffer.' If she were to marry Lord Warburton, she would find happiness, she thinks, in an 'unnatural' situation.

Although she persists in her idea that 'marriage is always a grave risk', Isabel finally decides to marry Osmond, tempted by the more elevated, exciting life that he can surround her with : travels, art, refinement. Established with her husband in a Roman palace, tasting the fruits of her new splendour, Isabel discovers shortly thereafter the dark, unhappy realities of marriage. Not only does she realize that Osmond (with the help of his old mistress, Mme Merle) is profiting from her immense fortune, but she recognizes his false personality : he is a pretentious, superficial, and debased adventurer. He has married Isabel for her money; he has never loved her; and now that his game is won, he inflicts upon her the daily torture of his rude judgements and negligence. Marriage, for Isabel becomes a nightmare. She is 'a woman who knew that she had thrown

away her life,' 'put into a cage', as if Osmond 'had locked her
into her room', '. . . she nevertheless assented to this intimation
that she too must march to the stately music that floated down
from unknown periods in her husband's past; she who of old
had been so free of step, so desultory, so devious, so much the
reverse of [the] processional. . . . When she saw this rigid system
close about her, draped though it was in pictured tapestries,
that sense of darkness and suffocation of which I have spoken
took possession of her; she seemed shut up with an odour of
mould and decay. She had resisted of course; at first very
humorously, ironically, tenderly; then, as the situation grew
more serious, eagerly, passionately, pleadingly! She had
pleaded the cause of freedom, of doing as they chose, of not
caring for the aspect and denomination of their life—the cause
of other instincts and longings, of quite another ideal. Then it
was that her husband's personality, touched as it had never
been, stepped forth and stood erect. The things she had said
were answered only by his scorn, and she could see he was
ineffably ashamed of her.'

Isabel faces, on the one hand, the conventional, stilted forms
that Osmond imposes upon their existence in the name of
elegance; on the other, her personality is being attacked, invaded, in her right to do and think as she pleases. Osmond
'wished her to have no freedom of mind', no freedom of experience; she understands that all the great, worthwile attainment she had sought is denied her by marriage. The restrictions
and tensions brought upon her by the constant interference
of Osmond, have a deep effect on her character. She is now
another person : no longer a curious and alive young woman,
eager to possess the world, but sad, resigned, marked by the
plight of her marriage.

In a stronger but allegorical fashion—and with intentional
exaggeration—James traces in *The Sacred Fount* the mysterious, malevolent influence of any intimate relationship on those
who love or are loved. Mrs Brissendeu, the heroine, is presented
as destroying the youth and vitality of her husband : she is
'eating poor Briss up inch by inch'. Although thirteen years

his senior, she appears younger than he; whenever they are together, this anomaly becomes increasingly apparent: '. . . he had been with her, however briefly, alone; and the intimacy of their union had been afresh impressed upon him. Poor Briss, in fine, looked ten years older.' But there are two other characters similar to the Brissendeus, Mary and Gilbert; but the positions are reversed: the man is domineering and possessive, whereas Mary is the 'sacrificed.' The influence and the exploration are here moral, not physical: Gilbert feeds on Mary's personality and intelligence, and his stupidity has turned to brilliance. As for Mary, who had been a calm and well-adjusted person, she is now increasingly nervous and dull. There would seem to be no real reciprocity and equality in love; the advantages and joys are possible only at the expense of one of the lovers. And so, the narrator-witness of *The Sacred Fount*, friend of the two couples, ends the story by saying that he 'had never seen before what consuming passion can make of the marked mortal on whom, with fixed beak and claws, it has settled as on a prey'.

For James, love and marriage are rendered even more dangerous when arranged to acquire purely social and material benefits: wealth, better class standing, professional advancement. They are treated then as mere scheme or strategy—as an evil intended exploitation or as a playful intrigue. Feelings as such seem to disappear. In his short novel, *The Awkward Age* (1898), James satirizes the upstarts of society for whom marriage is a convenient means to further ambition or redistribute possessions. The chase for a husband—the right one, i.e. the rich one—becomes a sophisticated game in the hands of mothers and daughters who fancy the same young men. Mrs Brooks a lively ingenious woman, deploys all her skill in planning to marry her daughter Nanda to Mitchy, a wealthy man, and thus help avoid the financial catastrophe which threatens the family. But the romantic Nanda does not lend herself to such manipulation: she is in love with Van, whom, unfortunately, her mother covets for herself. Van loves Nanda and would possibly marry her, but does not want 'to have the pecuniary

question mixed up with the matter' : too poor, always indeci-
sive, he will never declare his love. Mrs Brooks succeeds only in
imposing Nanda on the elderly Longdon, who will make her
a settlement. Throughout these successive incidents of match-
making and sentimental rivalry, real love never seems to appear,
only affections easily transferred from one person to another,
as the needs and interests of the moment dictate. If sincerity
manifests itself, as that between Nanda and Van, it is only
passive, to be quickly extinguished in the intrigues of a frivolous
society.

James spares his heroes and heroines true involvement in
love, but sometimes his secondary characters portray the passion
of love and are represented in the rôle of lovers. According to
him, the closeness of such associations must involve the threat
of possessive and destructive desires; love shared physically
would inevitably bring out in man his worst instincts : lovers,
when together, are 'dangerous—like some chemical combina-
tion' : Mme Merle and Osmond (*The Portrait of a Lady*), Kate
and Densher (*The Wings of the Dove*) and the Prince and
Charlotte (*The Golden Bowl*) provoke the unhappiness of
others, betray them unscrupulously to preserve their liaisons.
Their consciences are deadened, invaded by the sole pursuit
of selfish pleasure, and they become less agreeable, less human.
'You've not only dried up my tears, you've dried up my soul',
Mme Merele reproaches Osmond.

Physical love plays little part in James' novels; scenes of
passion are rare, and even these consist of hardly anything more
than a few furtive kisses. He lets it be thought that persons
unworthy of real respect abandon themselves to sensuality,
which he often identifies with moral depravity. Nevertheless,
toward the end of his life, he allows physical relations to play
a greater part in his works, whether because he had freed himself from the hesitancy to treat such matters or because of the
general fading out of Victorian prudishness. *A London Life*
(1888) and *What Masie Knew* (1897) are concerned with
promiscuity and adultery. *The Bostonians* hints discreetly at
sexual deviations : Miss Chancellor's affection for the young

Verena is of an ambiguous intensity; and in *The Pupil*, Morgan's attachment for his tutor is similarly suspect. In *The Turn of the Screw* one can see an examination of various aspects of sexual psychosis.

James seems to have gradually understood the dramatic, emotional impact of physical ties. But if he becomes increasingly direct, he still prefers to treat certain scenes metaphorically. An example may be found in *The Golden Bowl*, when Charlotte surrenders to the Prince's passion, a description both considerably vague and considerably suggestive: 'And so for a minute they stood together, as if strongly held and as closely confronted as any hour of their easier past even has seen them. They were silent at first, only facing and faced, only grasping and grasped, only meeting and met . . . then of a sudden, through this tightened circle, as at the issue of a narrow strait into the sea beyond, everything broke up, broke down, gave way, melted and mingled. Their lips sought their lips, their pressure their response and their response their pressure; with a violence that had sighted itself the next moment to the longest and deepest of stillnesses they passionately sealed their pledge.'

In avoiding any dramatized expression of intimacy, or simply in shying from sensuality, James shows himself incapable of separating the natural from the immoral aspect of lovemaking. And he seems to have overlooked—despite his fine capacity for converting and idealizing values—the purifying effects of love upon physical relationships, to the extent that they are no longer strictly physical. Probably, he was also influenced in such matters by the general circumspection of the times; most of his works appeared in periodical form in right-thinking American and English journals, and he was obliged to observe the customary reserve. He himself was aware of the restrictions imposed and complained that 'one can do so little with English adultery—it is so much less inevitable and so much more ugly in all its hiding and lying'. He regretted not writing for a French audience, for then 'the whole thing would be simple'.

On the other hand, from a simple aesthetic, literary point of view, James thought it necessary to avoid the commonplace

descriptions of sensuality and adultery found in certain novels
(and above all the French); he would not condescend to flatter
the instincts of the public, nor could he produce writing which
would be—and this was against his most natural tendency—
forthright and explicit. 'The carnal side of man appears the
most characteristic,' he said, 'if you look at it a great deal, and
you look at it a great deal if you do not look at the other'; 'I
think the exhibition of "Love" as "love"—functional love—
always suffers from a certain inevitable and insurmountable
flat-footedness . . . which is only to be counterplotted by
round-about arts—as by tracing through indirectness and tor-
turousities of application and effect—to keep it somehow interesting and productive (though I don't mean *re*productive!).'

For love to appear 'interesting and productive', James
examines it from a psychological viewpoint, revealing it as
essentially subjective. Motivated most frequently by a lack of
experience, by a vague sense of inadequacy, it appears in the
centre of the individual's consciousness, as a product of the
imagination, all satisfaction in reality being finally denied the
characters; it is a kind of solitary passion, a hidden force that
infects the alert and sensitive mind rather than the body and
the heart.

It is independent of its consummation, and even dissociated
from the loved one. The lovers are incapable of jealousy, and
in spite of their mutual sympathy or agreement, they are somehow not completely concerned and involved. They submit their
emotion to a process of interior transformation that solely
occupies them. They see the loved one through their illusions;
they lose their heart to an imaginary creature. Milly, in *The
Wings of the Dove*, loves Densher without really knowing him,
not speaking of love with him; her impressions from their
occasional meetings are enough to inspire in her the exaltation
she seeks. She lives and dies replete with her own dreams and
thoughts.

Aware of the friction between their contradictory feelings
of desire and reserve, the heroes' love develops as a process of
greater doubt and expectations, as a multiplied conflict of the

mind, sometimes swelling love to overpowering, distorted dimensions—which James finds exceedingly interesting (the main example is *The Turn of the Screw*). Indeed, love can become moral self-torture, but it can also espouse the forms of actual suffering. Seen as a beautiful process of longing and dreaming at first, it reaches almost too quickly the stage of disillusionment and despair; the imaginary process having attained intensity by its own momentum, inevitably goes into reverse: the hero recognizes the true nature of the loved one—generally deceitful—and comes to accept his congenial solitude. Milly allows herself to die when she realizes Densher's insincerity toward her and his attachment to Kate; Isabel's love turns to pain and disappointment from the moment Osmond reveals himself selfish and hypocritical. They will no longer be as before; their lives are at a standstill, and happiness will never exist.

All Jamesian heroes never know more than a few fleeting illusory moments of gratification. Love has been an escape: they have tried in vain to break out from their isolated condition, to deceive themselves into thinking that a change was possible, only to learn that, at the end, they will continue to live in the absence of love. Their greatest dream—in the rejection which they subconsciously carry—has been 'to be loved for oneself to be loved for myself', but this craving will be answered only by a deeper frustration. Not entirely, however, for their tragic situation—with no real settlement—ends in peace, in the submission to other more ambitious goals. Two Jamesian lovers, meeting after a separation of several years, understand once more—and all the more forcefully—'the vanity, the profanity, the impossibility of anything between them but silence'.

In James' works, love is not a sentimental affair. On one side, it is a tormented inner plight, while on the other, it represents in more violent terms man's conflict with the world and evil. The attitude of the lovers may be faint-hearted and egocentric, but love helps them reveal new possibilities of moral enrichment and becomes their main experience: an expansion of the self, a fruitful reorientation of the individual's consciousness. For Catherine, Isabel or Milly, it is a crisis which enables them to discover their true nature. James believes that not to love, although the outcome be deception, is equivalent to not living. The form under which love and passion appear is not the primary consideration, it is enough that they should be deeply felt : they are the means to a more intimate knowledge of people and things, to a more direct participation in existence. '. . . Those of us who love and know . . . , live so most,' he says. 'Any passion so great, so complete . . . is, satisfied or unsatisfied—a life.'

*The Beast in the Jungle* (1903), one of James' best-known short stories, introduces Marcher, who can neither love or live. He is a 'haunted man', carrying since his youth and deep within himself, an apprehension both exhilarating and disturbing, the 'sense of being kept for something rare and strange, possibly prodigious and terrible, that was sooner or later to happen to [him] . . . and that would perhaps overwhelm [him]'. He confides his secret to May, an affectionate, devoted friend of his, always interested in all that concerns him; now they await the great event together. '. . . The real form it should have taken . . . was the form of their marrying,' but Marcher 'put marriage out of the question.' He cannot admit that the 'great thing' in store for him 'amid the twists and turns of the months and years, like a crouching beast in the jungle' is love and nothing else. 'Tense and solemn', he thinks a more exceptional fate is reserved for him and allows the years to pass in expectation until he grows old : he never realizes—although his entire life is made of questioning and wondering—that May is passionately in love with him.

She has understood that Marcher's awaited destiny is to love and to be loved : 'Isn't what you describe,' she suggests to him at one point, 'perhaps but the expectation—or at any rate the sense of danger familiar to so many people—of falling in love?' Throughout the tale she never expresses her own feelings; she submits silently to her solitary longing. Marcher expresses consideration and kindness for her, but he never sees her as the woman he could love: 'That's it,' she tells him. 'It's what concerns me—to help you to pass for a man like another.' Abused more or less by him as a friend and a confidante, her rôle has been ambiguous: to pose as his wife or loved one, without becoming either. She gradually loses all hope, wastes away, and dies.

Later, when Marcher visits her grave, he meets in the cemetery a man who makes a profound impression on him: obviously also there to visit the grave of the woman he loved, his face bears the marks of real suffering, of a beautiful sadness at having known and lost true affection. Marcher understands then—too late—what *he* has missed: 'No passion had ever touched him . . . he had survived and maundered and pined but where had been *his* deep ravage? . . . The fate he had been marked for he had met with a vengeance—he had emptied the cup to the lees; he had been the man of his time, *the* man, to whom nothing on earth was to have happened. . . . The escape would have been to love her; then, *then* he would have *lived. She* had lived—who could say now with what passion—since she had loved him for himself; whereas he had never thought of her . . . but in the chill of his egotism and the light of her use.' This revelation—both ironical and tragic— concludes Marcher's trial and he dies in the cemetery from shock. He can not survive his newly acquired consciousness to have missed his chance—love in the person of May—and to face now the 'sounded void of his life'.

So with this story, James appears to assert—although abstractly again, only through Marcher's negative experience and belated, now useless, realization—the prime necessity of love for any human being who is to find self-fulfilment.

The complex—both fundamental and ambiguous—rôle of love in James' work can never be seen clearly without a reference to the author's life, his own hesitations—one might say, almost lack of interest—with regard to love. Of course, this theme encompasses many of the features of his work: his preference for moral values over physical manifestations, his ethic of self-denial and magnanimity, his timidity and, almost, perplexity about sexual matters. The general inadequacy which he shares with his heroes, resulted from a rejection by the others and an absence of love to the sense of his 'difference' and inner solitude. This situation, however, not only justifies his particular reserved attitude; it has also the retroactive effect: because of it, affection, sympathy, understanding, and companionship become all the more imperative, involving henceforth more than mere actual emotions of love.

Young women and orphans—in the deprivation of their youth or family—search feverishly and obstinately, for love and to be loved. This effort is not all too spontaneous or instinctive, it is rather a projection of the person as a whole—both will and conscience—to counter the threat of a void. Their love is a response to an insufficiency, an absence, and merges with their ever so stronger necessity to affirm, to justify themselves. Love is the only commitment—their only *attempt* toward a commitment. It rises and falls with violence, barely allowing each hero, as he so much wishes, to be loved for *what* he *is*, but only revealing him—in the appeal, then the refusal of love—for the one *he is*.

The heroes have an insurmountable fear of declaring their emotions, of transforming them into actions and decisions (the psychological process, or state, of being in love counting for them above all). Because, at the same time, love is part of a global, more important experience, they cannot at any moment come out of the narrow dwelling-place of their self-knowledge, their self-cohesion, and expect to surrender, to reach—what naturally any true love demands—self-abandonment. Their dilemma is insoluble desire and yet the impossibility of surrender. Moreover, they all share the conviction of a radical divorce between emotional and physical love, the latter representing a more irreversible—and to an extent, degrading—surrender. Not capable of freeing themselves from their highly-imaginative, self-centred minds, they can never approach the sphere of gratification, of sexual release, or even thought of temptation. These extremely reserved, cold attitudes do not seem real—this is not only explicable as the result of Victorian discretion (James transcends his times on so many other accounts)—and strikes the modern reader as one of the short-comings of James' work. Not that he should have ventured in some descriptive, realistic presentation of love-making, only that he should have been more exhaustive, more suggestive in this respect wherever his subject demanded it. I. W. Dupes writes that James, 'with all his wider experience, is more Puri-tan—if not simply less human—than Hawthorne'.

Jamesian love—essentially pure, ethereal, altruistic—can be defined at best as a search for an effective harmony : an ex-change of sensibilities and finer understanding, almost a com-plicity of being, a kind of total friendship. In this larger frame-work, love becomes a freer possibility, easily exceeding its own limits of desire, possession or jealousy. Closer to generosity, to pity, to affection, it becomes a purifying process, of itself with-in itself, always striving to attain new heights of sacrifice and abnegation : always far removed or gradually eliminating 'complications', it is finally a spiritual, absolute dimension. The Jamesian heroes love for the sake of loving—a luxury of the soul—and they do not require anything in return.

Despite the hidden force that drives one lover toward the other—with the resulting longing and conflict—they never escape their essential ambiguity : their inability to enter the realm of love, to cross the road that goes (without roundabout ways) from the 'I' to the 'other'. One is amused to see them, in presence of experience, revealing such an excessive reserve, such a constraint of self. Only in this aspect can one speak of abnormal tendencies or aberrations in James' works (as in him-self) i.e. the constant reverting to oneself—a narcissistic, intro-verted love, experienced only within the mind. To resolve the dilemma, one should be the possessor and the possessed at the same time, one should meet and love one's own double : only in this narrow sphere of self-sufficiency would one avoid the dangers of surrendering and preserve the sacred conscious totality of the individual.

James made himself the champion of impossible loves, of those doomed to silence, refusal and arrest : sometimes the obstacles are material and social, sometimes they proceed from the idealistic, exacting nature of love or from the many scruples, attentions and strains imposed by the heroes. Decidedly they prefer the situations of increasing difficulties, and their sentimental adventures move only in circles, revolving, until they return to their original vain, aspirations. The answer to this frustrating state is sublimation—parallel to James' preferred method of reversal and conversion. The impossible love— happily, fortunately, impossible—becomes the basis of transcendence and also, in Jamesian terms, of personal salvation. There is a *real* outcome, a clear manifestation, only they occur on another level: thrown back upon themselves, living in struggle and expectation, never fully loved and wanted (or only by those they like less), the heroes' love is a kind of self-contained explosion. Perhaps they have not known normal, ordinary happiness, but they have a happiness of their own, rarer, intrinsic, which is far from being negative. They find a more exalted feeling, a redoubled strife; they can reach the very limits of their beings—only because they have known self laceration in love, the wounds and the pains which leave deep scars in one's personality but also a considerable share of human experience. Therefore, through this duel-oriented, far-reaching love—as was the case with the confrontation of Europe or society oppression—the hero discovers a sense of purification and exaltation leading to his personal glory. The Jamesian ethics awards glory only on condition that nothing is gained *positively*, and that everything is lost.

# 8. Artists' Lives

AFTER THE social and international *élite*, the environment James knew best was undoubtedly the world of fine arts and letters. From his own experience, he had learned all about the joys and despair of creative pursuits; on the other hand, throughout his life he numbered many painters and writers among his friends. In his youth he had tried painting as a career, and later artistic sensibility would develop as a theme in his works. Many of his characters know how to use a brush; very often they are to be encountered in studios and museums, in cathedrals and palazzi, admiring beauty with an almost naïve veneration and, as often, associating with sculptors, painters and art collectors.

James is particularly concerned with the artist's life and problems in such novels and short stories as *Roderick Hudson*, *The Tragic Muse*, *The Liar* (1888), and *The Real Thing* (1893). He studies several aspects of the misunderstanding, the struggle between the artist and society: the interference of society with the artist's work, the value of his art (not generally that given to it by the public), the challenges and difficulties he encounters, the greater knowledge he obtains about the nature and the exigencies of his art. For example, in *The Real Thing* (a humourous long short story) a painter, commissioned to illustrate a fashionable novel, has as models Commander and Mrs Monarch, an impoverished couple who have neverthe-less retained the style and manners of high society. But they appear restrictive to the creative imagination, being too close to reality, 'the real thing but always the same thing'. Eventu-ally, the painter replaces them with his servant and a common girl because in his artistic transposition he sees them more like the hero and heroine of the novel : he has 'an inner preference for the represented subject over the real one', the subject that offers plastic, suggestive possibilities and allows him more room for 'the alchemy of art'. Willy-nilly, the Monarchs are compelled, for lack of money, to take the servant's place; in the final scene they serve tea and wash the dishes, while in the studio their rivals pose as a lady and a gentleman.

This story is a parable : James wishes to demonstrate that creation is divorced from literal imitation—that the relation between art and reality is much less obvious and far more intricate; that there is always a profound divergence between what the artist sees and what others see.

When his main character is a writer, James gives an even better representation of the conflict between the artist and the world : the writer's relationship with the public and the critics, his position in society and in the family. Although the cases selected for treatment are essentially tragic, they are conceived in the manner of light, entertaining allegories. James stresses the ironic, incongruous situations of the artist, who remains on the margin of social life and is often the plaything of everyday happenings and material conditions. Such heroes appear obsessed with their inner vision and the means of adequately expressing it through beauty. If they are selfish, it is because of their refusal to compromise their ideals, and their need to protect themselves from the repression and stupidity of others. They must accept the suffering and sacrifices inseparable from any vocation; their predicament is to live and to die in solitude.

According to *The Author of Beltraffio* (1884) 'life's really too short for art'. Instead of devoting himself to the demands of his work, he has to fight against his prudish wife's castigation of his writings as 'most objectionable' she lets their sick child die rather than see him read these works one day and be wrongly influenced. 'There is a hatred of art,' the novelist says, 'there's a hatred of literature—I mean of the genuine kinds. Oh the shams, those they'll swallow by the bucket !' His concern, of course, is not didactic morality, but "the attempt at perfection, the quest for which was to his mind the real search for the holy grail. . . .' Immorality lies in his failure truthfully to manifest his inspiration and be totally himself; he considers 'imperfections not only as an aesthetic but quite also as a social crime'.

The writer Dencome, in *The Middle Years* (1893), is doomed to a premature death; only now, 'at the very last', does he 'come into possession . . . of his art'. With a new assurance, in a few masterful strokes he dreams of unleashing finally his genius and forcing the public's recognition. But at the same time, he knows that it is too late and that all has been denied him : complete expression and perfection, he believes, can be achieved by no one : 'Oh, the pearl . . . is the unwritten. The pearl is the unalloyed, the *rest*, the lost ! . . . A second chance— *that's* the delusion. There never was to be one. We work in the dark—we do what we can—we give what we have. Our doubt is our passion and our passion is our task. The rest is madness of art.' In his forsaken state, alone and dying, he finds at least some comfort in his young doctor's sympathy and admiration : that one man could understand his intentions is enough to erase the public's long lasting apathy and convinces him that he has not created in vain. In this story, James stresses less the contrast between the artist's life and his immediate environ- ment than the struggles within himself and the general in- difference that surrounds him.

James is critical of authors who pander to the taste of the moment, whose ambition is success at any price. According to him, only work carried out in patience and silence, away from the clatter and the temptations of the world, guarantees an authentic artistic achievement : '. . . the only success worth one's powder was success in the line of one's idiosyncrasy. Consistency was in itself distinction, and what was talent but the art of being completely whatever it was that one happened to be?' But, James thought it unfortunate that the true artist should remain unrecognized. Critics and public seemed to praise and judge everything by trite, conventional measures—by any standard except that of the artist's dedication and the goal he

had attained; they more or less become involved with vulgariza-
tion, publicity and a blatant popular taste; they remain outside the realm of art, incapable of penetrating the mystery, the
torment of creation. In *The Next Time* (1893), James presents
two writers of dramatically opposed literary conceptions and
careers. Mrs Highmore, a fashionable blue-stocking, has published extremely successful works, which she knows to be worth-
less. Tired of her 'prolific course' she wishes—like her brother-
in-law, the obscure writer Limbert—to achieve 'if only once,
the same heroic eminence . . . an exquisite failure.' She tries
hard to fashion a masterpiece that will be spurned by the
general public and appreciated only by few connoisseurs, but
all she manages is another best-seller more widely acclaimed
and more vulgar than all her others. Limbert, an unrecognized
genius, has seen for years his fine, sensitive novels pass un-
noticed : now he is prepared to write the mediocre, sensational
work that will bring him fame and money. But all he can do
is to compose 'an unscrupulous, an unsparing, a shameless
merciless masterpiece'. He dies as he has lived, poor and unknown, while Mrs Highmore triumphantly pursues her career.

*The Figure in the Carpet* (1896) contains a more explicit
attack on 'our marked collective mistrust of anything like close
or analytical appreciation.' The great writer Vereker complains
that no one seriously cares to look for and comprehend the
essential theme, the 'buried treasure' of his books : '. . . the
peculiar thing, I've written my books most *for*. . . . It's the
finest, fullest intention of the lot, and the application of it has
been, I think, a triumph of patience, of ingenuity. . . . It
stretches . . . from book to book, and everything else, compara-
tively, plays over the surface of it. The order, the form, the
texture of my books will perhaps some day constitute for the
initiated a complete representation of it. So it's naturally the
thing for the critic to look for.'

Corvick and his wife, critics in their own right, set out to
discover the 'figure in the carpet' in Vereker's works. After
many wonderings and disappointments, Corvick succeeds in
finding what it might be, but he dies suddenly before imparting

his knowledge to anyone except his wife, who now refuses to disclose it; a novelist herself, she 'used' it in her writings, 'lived' by it—as we learn after her own death.

Vereker's death, in the meantime, necessitates a new search for the essential meaning of his books. In fact, he 'never took the smallest precaution to keep it secret'; simply, readers and critics do not make the effort to perceive it, to understand it : his message continues waiting—brilliantly delineated through the magic of style—for someone to seek it out and believe in it.

In this story, James not only expresses his dissatisfaction with superficial criticism, and the possessive annexation—the private use, so to say—that sometimes it makes of the author's intentions. He is concerned as well with the nature of art, which not merely expresses reality, even in its widest range, but also creates a particular means—or Style—for expressing reality. Not so much meaning and ideas are implied in the symbolism of 'the figure in the carpet' as structural modulations which—like a pattern or leitmotiv—stand out to guide and illuminate meaning and ideas.

If James regrets the obscurity and solitude in which great talents are often condemned to live, he regrets the heavy burden of recognition and celebrity bestowed (not always justly) upon the happy few. Whatever the case, the world refuses to understand that 'a great work needs silence, privacy, mystery'. Of the renowned authors, public and critics are less eager to learn about their art's real qualifications than to pry into their habits, past and private lives. They stifle them with adulation and intrusions. According to James, 'the artist's life's his work, and this *is* the place to observe him. What he has to tell us he tells us with *this* perfection. . . . The best interviewer is the best reader. . . . Admire him in silence, cultivate him at a distance and secretly appropriate his message.'

James' account of the misadventures of the writer in society is not without a certain playful, spiteful charm. In the case of *The Death of the Lion* (1894), the story is both comic and tragic. Paraday, a talented novelist to whom public praise has long been due, by chance suddenly becomes the author of the day : 'He's beset, badgered, bothered—he's pulled to pieces on the pretext of being applauded. People expect him to give them his time, his golden time, who wouldn't themselves give five shillings for one of his books.' Dazed by so much agitation, 'squeezed into this horrible age', he finds himself far removed from his 'monastic life', realizing that 'success was a complication and recognition had to be reciprocal'. He nourishes a 'passionate desire to be left to finish his work', but sees himself instead fêted and dragged here and there, as the 'lion' of London socialites and, in particular, as the showpiece of Mrs Wimbush, 'a violent force', 'proprietress of the universal menagerie'. Exhausted and resigned to his fate, he falls sick and dies during a weekend party, while his last work—unfortunately still unfinished—is mislaid by his fashionable admirers, who are already hot in pursuit of other literary idols.

James goes as far as to believe that to produce a worthy work of art, the artist should despise success, money and society, that he should even renounce his private life and personal happiness—the pleasures of marriage and a family. This Jamesian conviction receives clear expression in *The Lesson of the Master* (1892). The English writer Saint-George is no longer able to compose books of inspired intensity as he desires : to satisfy his wife's social ambition and elegant pretences, and to provide for his sons' future, he is compelled to earn more and more money. He must produce popular best-sellers at great speed, whereas his wife is careful to destroy those of better literary merit, because they would sell poorly. Every morning she shuts him in his windowless study—'a good big cage'—where he is 'walled into his trade'. He thinks of himself as a 'successful charlatan', being alone in the realization that, although society and the critics might admire him unceasingly, his novels are now devoid of artistic value.

He meets a talented young writer, Overt, who is in love with a Miss Fancourt and wants to marry her. To protect him from a fate similar to his own Saint-George warns him against the dangers of marriage : 'I've got everything in fact but the great thing . . .', he says.'The sense of having done the best—the sense which is the real life of the artist and the absence of which is his death, of having drawn from his intellectual instrument the finest music that nature had hidden in it, of having played it as it should be played. He either does that or he doesn't— and if he doesn't he isn't worth speaking of. . . . Well, all I say is that one's children interfere with perfection. One's wife interferes. Marriage interferes. . . . Try to do some really good work. . . . Well, you can't do it without sacrifices—don't believe that for a moment . . . I've made none, I've had everything. In other words I've missed everything. . . . The artist—the artist! Isn't he a man all the same?

'I mostly think not. You know as well as I what he has to do : the concentration, the finish, the independence he must strive for from the moment he begins to wish his work really decent. . . . To *do* it—to do it and make it divine—is the only thing he has to think about. . . . He has nothing to do with the relative—he has only to do with the absolute, and a dear little family may represent a dozen relatives. Then you don't allow him the common passions and affections of men?

'Hasn't he a passion, an affection, which includes all the rest? Besides, let him have all the passions he likes—if only he keeps his independence. . . . [He] can produce his effect only by giving up personal happiness.'

Overt accepts the 'lesson of the master'. He travels abroad for some time and tries to forget Miss Fancourt; free to work at will, he soon writes a new masterpiece. However, when he returns to England, he finds Saint-George (whose wife had died in the meantime), about to marry Miss Fancourt. He wonders now whether he has not been duped by Saint-George but, the great writer explains to him, a trifle desultorily and unconvincingly, that he is marrying again because not being a true artist, he has decided to stop publishing.

This particular story—to some extent more than the preceeding tales—is presented as a fable; the prevalent tone is humorous, the situations ludicrous, the ideas often eccentric. James is writing allegories, experimenting with deliberately exaggerated approaches and illustrations, but without claiming them as objective and conclusive, and hardly sharing the far-fetched, anomalous opinions he explores. Nevertheless, these stories contain a number of autobiographical details and typic- ally Jamesian concerns about the artist's relation to his art and to the world—concerns which sprang from his long awaited recognition by the public and his existence of laborious celibacy on one hand, of mounting sociability on the other. Throughout his life he had been something of an *artiste maudit*, for—out- growing the realism and sentimentalism in vogue at that time— he had explored areas yet unknown in literature and which remained misunderstood, if not by-passed, by contemporary criticism. He had to justify the path he had chosen, his par- ticular—estranged—situation. The ensuing tension, and con- flict in his career were expressed psychologically in his major novels and in an episodic, anecdotal manner in his tales. There, he contrasts the notions of success and perfection : on the one hand, the secret desire for the public's reward of sympathy and interest, with all the impositions and profanation that this implies; on the other, the urge to achieve in seclusion and silence, away from worldly temptations (always more or less vulgar in James' eyes) an intense and truthful body of work. He reaffirms his devotion to beauty, his belief in the durability of art; he opposes a dual aesthetic—ascetic ideal to the material, transistory values of celebrity and happiness. And so he reverses the dictates of his own fate : by choosing himself to be the writer who spurns publicity and success, money and private pleasures, and preferring the tormented trials of his art. More specifically, toward the end of his career, he emphasizes the 'struggle' of authors against ill-considered criticism and bad taste, against the preposterous demands of a modern world dominated by mass-media, competition and fashion. He often portrays a 'small tragedy of the *vie littéraire*', in which the two main enemies are 'the age of trash triumphant' and the 'yoke', 'a kind of hell' of personal obligations and mundanities. The writer can never win against the flood of time and pressure; he longs in vain for 'an extension', 'another go' in order to per- severe for good or rather to rediscover the 'revelation of his range', his 'transcendant illusions'. But all he has to contend with, after the sacrifices and useless protests, is the feeling of 'some felt embarrassment, some extreme predicament of the artist enamoured of perfection, ridden by his idea or paying for his sincerity'.

Ultimately James is convinced that the artist is an exceptional person—a creature apart—and that there is a lasting incompatibility between commitment for the sake of art and a search for happiness: the artist cannot serve two masters. It would be difficult and pointless to defend James' questionable stand in these matters: it is relevant only as far as it illustrates the novelist's own drama and the conflict between man and the world—as we find it in his other works—but given here in a sharply outlined context of specific professional purpose and conditions. From *Roderick Hudson* to *The Death of the Lion*, throughout his life as a writer, James hardly varied this theme; therefore, the artist emerges from among his different character types as a hero of modern life in constant battle with his own times, eluding facility and moral decay, fallacious enjoyments and everyday domesticity. His affirmation is expressed not in action but in creation. James wished to portray the tragic dichotomy which is the fate of the real artist: a refusal to live in the world in order to live fully in the work of art.

# 9 The Sense of the Past

HENRY JAMES' interest in life does not evolve solely in a present-to-future dimension. He is also concerned with all 'wasting life' —with the lost forever or the 'might have been'. This introduces his characters to another psychological expansion, for they are not recalling their past existence. Rather, they speculate on what they were unable to achieve (but could have achieved): 'nostalgically misplaced and disconnected' they indulge in 'possibilities of recognition and reciprocity'. Their search for 'the sense of the past' can easily become an hallucination.

James was, however, sensitive to the surviving, continuously present marks of the past, his native country being devoid of long and rich traditions. Like him, his heroes are always attracted by the centuries-old accumulations of art, history, customs: the dense, varied European setting where most of their actions occur. We see them move through ancestral homes and art galleries, admiring aristocracy and civilization, having a particular liking for 'spoils' and 'everything old', for household curios and half-faded portraits. These attributes, being interwoven into their very psychology and adventure, extend the limits of their contemporary life, draping them—so to say —in the imposing costume of the age, bringing out a note of permanence in their incongruous, unstable world. The back-cloth of the past depends but little on actual description and realistic precision: it is never given *per se*, but as a multiplied poetic and suggestive presence looming in the background, sufficiently close, sufficiently explorable to stimulate the imagination. The unfinished novel, *The Sense of the Past*, goes back a century in time, but James never attempts a detailed presentation of that period : he generally does not exceed the time of his youth and the limits of his own memory : 'I delight,' he writes, 'in a palpable, imaginable, *visitable* past—in the . . . marks and signs of a world we may reach over to . . . the poetry of the thing outlived and gone.'

James is deeply aware of the inviolable aspect of the past which one should continue to respect and preserve. No documentation, no applied reconstruction can be more truthfully revealing than the general, more or less vague, evocative impressions. He satirizes the vain, preposterous research that tries to break the sealed past or any complacent admiration that reduces its complexity to simplified, face-value images. Only through secret intimations, rapid snatches—in an inner illumination of the spirit—can one discover the essential flavour, the *sense* of the fully unreachable past.

The hero of *The Aspern Papers* (1888) wishes to gain access to the distant memories of Miss Bordereau, who had been once the mistress of the great poet Jeffery Aspern (Shelley). He covets in particular her letters from Aspern, convinced to secure thus a complete explanation of the poet's private life and personality. A mysterious incarnation of the past, the old lady is represented symbolically with her eyes hidden : she is wearing 'a horrible green shade which served for her almost as a mask'. The past is suddenly revealed to him—not in the drawers that he goes so far as to force—in her eyes when, on one occasion, she removes her shade. He recognizes the only truth worth knowing beyond any trivial detail : the real and deep love that existed between Aspern and herself.

In *The Birthplace* (1903) James exercises his irony on the public adulation of manuscripts, portraits and relics of all kinds which belonged to a famous English poet (Shakespeare). Gredge, the custodian of the poet's birthplace, who for years has lived in the presence of these abundant mementos—who so brilliantly, dramatically explains them to the visitors—concludes that they hardly represent the great man's real past. Only by reading and re-reading the poet's works, by letting his mind freely speculate on conjectures and possibilities, is he able to imagine the reality : 'I'm interested,' he says, 'in what I think is the interesting thing . . . the eternally fermenting one. The fact of the abysmally little that, in proportion, we know . . . what there must have been . . . what in fact there is to wonder about.'

The preceding stories concern the rediscovery of remote events and dead persons—a reality which did exist in one way or another, although its representation can never be complete. James shows the indirect approach of inner revelation—through perception, not knowledge—provoked by a sudden sensation, a fleeting grasp of the outside world, the subconscious memory. His own *Memoirs*, written at the end of his life, are characteristically nebulous and anachronistic, recapturing not so much specific events, places or people, but an overall atmos-phere, which none the less appears successful as an evocation of his youth : he defines the result as a 'magic cluster of associa-tions'. A critic has justly remarked that his 'sense of the past' was nothing else than 'the sense of a sense'. James' exploration, therefore, can be compared to Proust's as far as it relies also on unexpected, effortless starts of recognition, on association and relation, and as far as it is guided, renewed by mere occasional half-irrelevant, half-forceful suggestions from reality; on the whole, it is removed from Proust's exploration and his philo-sophical theory on memory and time. Moreover, in his later works, James deliberately eliminates the direct confrontation with the past—as a past which actually existed.

His treatment of this theme will become more psychological, closer to a product of the sensibility and the imagination, more concerned with a vision of possibilities missed, with a life which could have existed, but never did. The heroes, conscious of a void, of a failure in their present state, conscious above all that it is *too late* for them to expect anything from the future, con-struct within themselves—on the basis of what has been—the supposition of what might have been : a plausible though lost existence and identity. In many cases, their experience verges on obsession.

In *The Beast in the Jungle*, for example Marcher is 'a haunted man'—haunted by the emptiness of his life, by the death of the woman whom he did not know how to love, by the feeling that 'at this time of day, it was simply, it was overwhelmingly too late'. Before he dies, his only consolation is 'to live entirely with . . . his unidentified past . . . to win back by an effort of thought the lost stuff of consciousness'. 'Thus in short he settled to live—feeding all on the sense that he once had lived and depended on it not alone for a support but for an identity.' He is trying to explore, therefore, not so much his memories, his forlorn, uncompletely lived joys, as 'his *recovering* of the Dead Self'.

In 1905, when on a visit to America after an absence of almost a quarter of a century, James found his country entirely transformed, having retained only a few traces of life as he knew it during his earlier years. This sense of a past, surviving only in the consciousness of those who belonged to it, was inspiration of the stories *Crapy Cornelia* (1909) and *The Jolly Corner* (1909), whose heroes look in modern New York for the remaining signs of their own vanished youth. In the first, White-Mason prefers the company of his fiancée (much younger than he and incapable of his recollections) to that of his old friend Cornelia. 'Conscious, ironic, pathetic survivors together of a dead and buried past', they can—in the same compassion—worship their 'lost world' before the 'very altar of memory'. We do not know if they are actually trying to relive any distant personal happenings; we only see them joined in a vision of their common, shared past.

In *The Jolly Corner*, Brydon, returning to New York after thirty years abroad, is eager to recover 'the spirit . . . of the better time', the 'presences of the other age'. A lady whom he once knew and who now becomes his friend is the only one to understand his longing—for she is secretly in love with him. However, rather than this sentimental attachment, his ritual visits to the old empty family house help him recapture his reminiscences—by strange assumptions and almost frightened appeals. At night, walking from room to room, he loses himself in 'the depths of the house of the past, of that mystical other world that might have flourished for him'. So, not at any moment is he searching to revive exactly what he knew; he only listens to the humming of the past, its silent message through the years : he enters into an 'absurd speculation', eventually meets his ghostly double, his American self that might have been had he not left the country. 'It comes over to me,' he says, 'that I had then a strange *alter-ego* deep down somewhere within me. . . .'

James' last unfinished novel, *The Sense of the Past* (1917), is also concerned with such a division of the protagonist's identity on this extended dimension of the past. The subject, writes James, is '. . . the exchange of identity between my young American of today and his relative of upwards of a hundred years ago . . .; face to face with my tremendously engaged and interested hero is the *alter-ego* of a past generation of his "race". . . . It is himself who looks out recognizingly *at* himself.'

Ralph, an American historian, has a 'natural passion for everything old'; having inherited his ancestors' house in London, he is all too anxious to visit it. There, among other things, he discovers an unusual portrait : the man represented is turned away and his back is all that can be seen. Ralph is fascinated and continually returns to the portrait. In a curious, hallucinating scene, the painted figure reveals his face : Ralph then finds himself in the presence of his 'self' of the year 1820. This ancestor, who always has been obsessed by the future, is now happy to establish this contact with him and proposes to assume his present identity, while Ralph undertakes to live the other's past. He can satisfy in this way 'his desire to remount the stream of time'. 'No man, he well believed could ever so much have wanted to look behind and still behind.'

James is not interested in the simple exchange of personalities and corresponding surprise effects, but rather in the 'double consciousness, the representation of which makes the thrill and the curiosity of the affair, the consciousness of being the other and yet himself also, of being himself and yet the *other* also'. This is Ralph's true adventure of rediscovering the past—the simultaneous possession of his two personalities—not so much the experiencing of probable events. However, in accepting the painted figure's past, he has also accepted the man's obsession of the future : Ralph is haunted now by his new identity and he seeks an escape in the future, in the person he was at the beginning of the story. 'If his idea in fine was to recover the lost moment, to feel the stopped pulse, it was to do so as experience in order to be again consciously the creature that he had been, to breathe as he had breathed and feel the pressure that he had felt.'

If the 'sense of the past' is not a dominant theme in James' works, it is none the less one of the most intriguing. Not only is the treatment psychological—the evocation of reminiscences or a century-old cultural background, communicated through the heroes' perceptions—but it is increasingly linked to the obscure, intermittent, rôle of the imagination. James would seem to be one of the first to explore this theme less as a recapturing of the past than as a possible derangement of the mind.

The characters do not have so much recourse to the real 'poor dear extinct past', but above all to 'what might have been' : they dwell on 'the feeling of an occasion missed'. Therefore their 'escapade', their 'miraculous excursion in the past' changes into a struggle with the Time—now measurable and experienced, now imagined and extensible—of their own vital dimension of Present-Past-Future. Through this 'past, invoked, invited, encouraged', they enlarge and enrich their present inadequate condition; they acquire the sense of having intensely lived before and, finally, by a strange co-ordination in their mind, of 'cultivating [their] sense of the future'. For them, indeed present and past, past and present, are inseparable (the past is seen as an extension of the present, of which consciousness is never lost), and on the other hand, at the very same moment they also exist in a related future : they desire a 'self-projection', to become 'somebody else', to find again the 'missing link' of unity and fullness, 'really almost reaching out in imagination—as against time—for something'. This peculiar exploration stems from some deep regret, some long dissatisfaction; in their purely subjective reality it becomes for them the only means of restoring their equilibrium, of outgrowing the sense of wasted, missed experience : this enables them to 'live with an intensity unprecedented' in the wider range of 'the real duration' Ironically enough, it is only in going *backward* that they come to 'a sort of victory' of themselves over themselves and over the 'boundaries of life'. In the process of discovery, they are not subject, however, to any liberating exaltation; on the contrary they feel increasingly 'immersed and shut in, lost and damned'; finding themselves more on uncertain ground, they are haunted by their experience—by the fears from the unreachable past. One could almost say that there is an 'obsession' with the 'obsession'. On the other hand, their recaptured past is always *temps perdu*, since it is composed of non-existent, secretly-denied identities or of—more or less— probable and contrived trials. It occurs only as a mental speculation, as a revelation in the subsconscious mind.

James' 'sense of the past' appears as an attempt to destroy the division and sub-divisions of measurable time, which are irrelevant to the freely evolving flow of imagination and consciousness. He wishes to extend the frontiers of man's time-limited existence by including not only the remembered life, but also the regrets, wondering, credible eventualities, and impossible dreams that man fashions in relation to his past and future : what has been lived he unites with the unknown— the true with the imaginary. 'The sense of the past' has a distinctly obsessive and gratuitous aspect; it is closely related, therefore, to James' 'ghost stories'.

# *10. The Supernatural*

THERE WAS a long tradition of weird experiences in the novelist's family: his father, his brother William and his sister Alice had all at some time received the visitation of an unreal, unusual presence and a subsequent sensation of fear and help-lessness. James himself had had his 'immense hallucination'— a dream in which he fought and then pursued a mysterious spectre. In addition, his father was greatly concerned with the supernatural world, William speculated on the unconscious and on spiritualism, and there were the general influences of Hawthorne and Poe, the mesmerism fashionable at the time or later, the psychological research of Charcot. First in his youth, and then toward the end of the century—his interest in the subject renewed—James wrote a small number of 'ghost stories' dealing with strange apparitions and obsessions. This was his way into the world of the subconscious, allowing a glimpse of the 'supernatural element' in earthly life; he intro-duces in his stories an element of fantasy and nightmare, com-bining 'ambiguity' and 'awkwardness', 'mysteries and secrets'.

Some phantoms appear to the living, whereas others remain invisible and interfere indirectly; some are shapes of terror and revenge, whereas others are well-meaning and protective. The heroine of *The Romance of Certain Old Clothes* (1868), for example, is overwhelmed by the shadow of her husband's first wife for having wished to violate the memory of their marriage. In *The Real Right Thing* (1899), the writer Doyne intervenes, after his death, in the work of his biographer, makes letters and documents disappear and finally prevents him from enter-ing the study, where all his papers are kept. In both these cases, the spirits are hostile or malevolent. Others, although they bring about a certain *malaise*, are peaceful presences, fantastic 'quasi-supernatural' figures, like those in a fairy-tale. For example, in the story *Nona Vincent* (1892), the dramatist Wayworth is visited in a dream by the heroine of his latest play : this vision calms his fears about the interpretation of the part by the actress who will play it. In *The Friends of the Friends* (1896), a man joyfully welcomes each night the apparition of the woman whom he would have liked to meet; now he falls in love with her spirit and commits suicide in the hope of joining her.

James is not concerned with ghosts, pure and simple, who act of their own volition and whose interventions cannot be explained. He does not dissociate them from the mental states of those whom they haunt, generally representing them as the results of 'some great and constant trouble', of ' "unnatural" anxiety, a *malaise* so incongruous and discordant'. They express suppressed desires, recurrent preoccupations, remorse, or, as in *The Jolly Corner* and *The Sense of the Past*, they can be the 'double personality'—an apparition of the self to the self, a symbolic representation of a man's 'alternate identities'. The heroes seem almost to undergo a psychoanalytic probing; their adventures, as related, are the imprinted images of their deepest individual disturbances. James admits searching, in each case, for the 'unconscious obsession' !

This relationship between the spectres and the psychological content, James will emphasize in almost all of his supernatural tales. In *Owen Wingrave* (1892), the hero would seem to have been killed by the ghost of an ancestor as a punishment for having soiled the family honour : he had refused to follow a military career. But he does not *see* the ghost : if he himself believed in it, to defy it, this occurred only in his own troubled mind. The tale is more a development of the theme of 'a transmitted hereditary, mystical, almost supernatural force . . . in the life and consciousness of a descendant'. Owen is the victim of his own dilemma of conscience, his regrets and 'worries' : 'strange voices . . . that seem to mutter at [him]—to say dreadful things. . . .' Similarly, in *Nona Vincent*, Wayworth sees the imaginary phantom of his heroine because he is involved in a 'particular complication of anxieties'. Brydon, in *The Jolly Corner*, eventually confronts his other self, because this constitutes a 'particular form of surrender to his obsession' with the past. More characteristic is *Sir Edmund Orme* (1891), in which Mrs Marden and her daughter's fiancé each see Sir Edmund's ghost. Mrs Marden is filled with remorse about Sir Edmund's suicide (she refused to marry him and now she fears that his ghost might revenge her daughter.) The fiancé is visited by the same apparition, but because he is tortured by the woman he loves—as Sir Edmund had been. The spectre seems to protect and encourage him whereas he threatens Mrs Marden : he is nothing more than the reflection of the two characters' feelings.

*The Turn of the Screw* (1898) is the masterpiece among James' supernatural tales. Complex in nature, it lends itself to varied interpretations; a large number of opposed judgements have been made of its more specific psycho-analytical intention. The author himself defines it as a 'queer dim play of consciousness', as a 'deep well of unconscious cerebration'. The heroine is a simple and innocent young woman, governess of two orphans, Flora and Miles, aged ten and twelve, whom their uncle has entrusted to her with the request that he be left untroubled. Her lack of experience, on one hand, her growing conscientiousness, on the other, as a teacher and mistress of the lonely country house where she lives with the children, cause her to imagine her tasks to be more arduous than they are.

The recollection of the somewhat outlandish, intriguing uncle —guardian of the children—whom she had met only once, but who, in all probability, had made a strong impression on her, recurs with an obsessive frequency in her imagination. For instance, while out for a stroll she conjures with the thought that 'someone would appear there at the turn of a path and would stand before me and smile and approve'. Indeed, a few days later, she is confronted by the apparition of the valet— once in charge at the house—who had died before her arrival :

curiously enough, he is dressed in his master's clothes. From this moment, the intensity of the hallucination increases and she also encounters the ghost of her predecessor as governess. When alone with Flora or Miles, she senses the presence of 'another person . . . a figure of . . . unmistakable horror and evil'. She supposes—unjustifiably—that the governess and the valet were lovers, that they perverted the children's innocence and that now, their haunting presence has the same lascivious, corrupt intention. She is more convinced that the children see them too, that they are in some kind of complicity with them. Although the apparitions are vividly portrayed, James never indicates whether Flora and Miles are in fact aware of them or not.

The governess is the narrator of her own story. In this fashion, all reality is refracted in her mind, and we penetrate only *her* visions. She imagines more than she observes; and her imaginings she transposes into deductions, apprehensions, and finally, the certainty of facts. Fantasy is turned to reality : henceforth she can invent anything, believe anything; she is surrounded by 'depths, depths' : 'The more I go over it the more I see in it, and the more I see in it the more I fear. I don't know what I *don't* see—what I don't fear !'

Too many forces are prying upon her : in her solitary feeling, living in the isolated estate, dreaming about the children's uncle, she undergoes an interior crisis of love frustration and sexual repressions—which joined to her naturally morbid and alert mind—provoke her speculation with the unknown, the apparitions she sees, the terror she feels, the depravity of the ghostly figures and the children . . . and also other much darker possibilities that escape her grasp. All this points to her general instability, her troubled inadequacy. Sometimes her hallucination borders on madness; she reaches such a stage of mental frenzy that, in her turn, she becomes the source of obsession and terror for the children and almost of corruption of their innocence. Flora falls sick and Miles dies in her arms.

James' method here is deliberately tortuous and obscure. The insights he tries to reach spread in several directions before finally converging into a sort of unfathomable exploration which is frightening in itself. No ghosts are really necessary: but there are many subtle hints of man's evil impulses. The young governess becomes almost a temptress to Miles and wishes, perhaps, to pervert him. In advancing so far on such perilous, constantly misleading grounds, James strikes a daring, original note and foreshadows modern psychological research and the use of the stream of consciousness technique.

His supernatural tales become fascinating reading because they never depart from the real world and are never implausible. The external development remains meticulously natural, and the spectres do not seem to disturb it: they are represented as integral, as feasible phenomena. Moreover, they never have fantastic attributes; their physical aspect, dress and poise, are those of human beings who can easily be mistaken for real persons. They are truly the re-incarnation of more abstract subjective realities.

James believes that 'a good ghost story must be connected at a hundred points with the common objects of life'; he is in search of only 'the strange and sinister embroidered on the very type of the normal and easy'.

But at the same time, these tales communicate a 'sensation of horror' and of 'oppression'. Without the conventional effects of the ghost story, James creates a psychological hallucinatory tension. His characters merely act under particular stresses and pressures, often in trying, troubled circumstances. They themselves add the element of horror by means of the strange occurrences in their unbound, irrepressible mental ·build-up. The psychology of James' heroes is no longer a mere series of motivations and reactions, subtle or vivid, more or less articulate and explicable. Now, as in his theme of 'the sense of the past', he tries to include the unexpressed side of mental complexity—dreams or obsessions—that remains in the background of 'actual life' and suggests the extended imaginative powers of the human consciousness. He remarks on the intricate play of hallucination and reflection, of the spontaneous inventions of the mind and its deliberate additions—as if, in a semi-somnolent state, these characters were both dreaming and helping themselves dream. Without clear division between the applied and voluntary mental process, between conscious and sub-conscious, James proceeds with an analysis of the inexpressible and the unavoidable, where the heroes sink helplessly (but sometimes with a secret delight) in the shadowy depths of their personalities. They enter into terrifying and delirious states, domains of pure conjecture—always closer to apprehension than explanation—where they no longer possess any fixed identity. For James, the supernatural is a kind of intangible psyche, offering further extension of the individual. Alien and superior forces do not intervene; the spectres are only symbolic utterances of inner troubles and derangements.

The heroes are attracted and fascinated by their experience; they discover a 'strong appeal', a kind of 'mystic initiation' that enables them to pass beyond their immediate consciousness of the real world and enjoy 'the possibility of an intercourse closer than that of life'. This is the extreme result—beneficial, exor-cising, liberating—of their haunting obsessions.

Endowed, like some of his characters, with peculiarly 'dis-tinct intuitions', 'mysterious powers', 'a supersubtle sixth sense', James tries to gain 'accessibility to forms of life . . . command of impressions, appearances, contacts, closed . . . to the rest of us'. He wishes to explore the hidden world of evidence that lies behind individual consciousness; in this way human destiny no longer exists as something restricted to its own limits, but in relation to other factors—fatality, death or immortality.

*      *

James writes of an 'occult power' controlling the lives of men, whose presence is felt only as a suggestion, as an apprehension. Some of his novels contain an inexorable sense of fate—apparent in the consciousness of his characters. They seem to have an inner knowledge of it—through the self-condemnation which frequently accompanies their trials—and even to be acting in accordance with it, so much do they indulge in the imperative demands of their human nature and condition.

Always engaged in struggles with themselves and with decisive happenings, they are subject to a kind of moral determinism and live on the eve of a final, inexorable fate.

In James' novels there is no random distribution of events and no real psychological freedom. The heroes wish to change their lives and enrich their personalities, but from the start they are bound by certain norms and prescriptions which will remain the same throughout their adventures and downfall; they never really escape from their Americanism and idealism, their high cosmopolitan society, or their tragic solitude and absence of love. The vanity of their attempts at liberation is made more obvious by their moral predestination. They are doomed to remain what they are; their only freedom is to be able to reach the utmost boundaries of self. Never leaving this deterministic basis of progression, without ultimate evasion, their predicaments are of value only because they are directed toward the realization of their own destinies.

Many of James' plots rely on a sudden reversal, implying the intervention of a superior law of justice and retribution. Sometimes, the actions evolve beyond the heroes' control; and contradict almost point by point what, at first, they calculated and hoped for. Thus, a close relationship is established between their decisions and the consequences. Finally, the complete reversal of situations suggest their possible justification or their punishment. In the story symbolically entitled *The Wheel of Time* (1892), Maurice abandons Fanny, the woman who loves him. Twenty years later, his daughter is deserted by the young man whom *she* loves, and who happens to be Fanny's son : unhappy, miserable, she dies from a broken heart. In this way Maurice is punished for his original desertion. In the story *Sir Dominic Ferrand* (1892), Peter Baron has acquired the compromising letters of a famous man—Sir Dominic. Whenever he is about to publish them, Mrs Ryves, with whom he is in love, shuns him; whenever he is hesitant about publishing them, she welcomes him. She knows nothing about the correspondence, while Peter does not know that she is Sir Dominic's illegitimate daughter. Since there are no ghosts nor apparitions in this tale, how could one explain the 'occult power' that intervenes? What is the connexion between the two characters, between their actions and their future destiny?

James seems to believe in an imminent judgment to which human actions and merits are subject: a righteousness that punishes and rewards. Hence, his predilection for certain para-doxes—*splendid* failures or *vulgar* successes—and the opposi-tion between ultilitarian and absolute values: in order to emphasize that our desires and decisions are inadequate for mastery of the complex mathematics of fate. In many cases, he shows that some people may lose on the level of fortune and happiness, but that their defeat and abandonment can ultimately—in an unexpected way, by virtue of the intensity with which they have lived and failed—allow them a greater enrichment of consciousness. The losers are often the winners. James' works leave us with an impression that the ways of fate are unforeseeable, that they are outside of the individual's will and restricted comprehension. Every hero would seem to find self-fulfilment to the degree that he gradually lets himself go and accepts the intangible power within himself. This power will guide him to an eventual meaning of which he was hither-to ignorant, not so much with regard to life itself or his actions, but in relation to his own absolute permanency as being. There-fore, each protagonist travels a dual road: that of his desired achievement in the world, and that of the spiritual results of living. The two ways are sometimes contradictory, and failure on the first is accompanied by moral triumph on the second.

Here precisely we encounter that notion of fate or intensi-fied individual consciousness which for James is the way to survival—the eternal realization of the 'I'. When examining James' works, it is not possible to talk of divine providence on one hand, or any purely human positivity on the other; be it as it may, the characters unwittingly follow an inexorable forward movement—a call that they *must* answer—as if nothing were in vain, everything had a purpose, and all were made clear in a dimension other than that of human volition and under-standing.

Death in James' novels is rarely accidental; it does not necessarily imply the end of everything. Frequently, it would rather appear to be the accomplishment of human destiny and, even more, the prolongation of life. 'Why do we make such an ado about death? What is it, after all, but a sort of refinement of life?' The death of Milly Theale, for instance, is in itself a survival—although there is no question of existence for the heroine in another world. James is also concerned with what one critic has called the theme of 'death-in-life'; he attempts to achieve a fusion of the two states—to prove that death can also be made the means of life.

His story *The Altar of the Dead* (1895) offers the most characteristic example. Strausom's worship of his departed friends is for him a real reason for being alive : '. . . it had come to him early in life that there was something one had to do for them. They were there in their simplified, intensified essence, their conscious absence and expressive patience, as personally there as if they had only been stricken dumb. They asked for so little that they got poor things, even less, and died again, died every day, of the hard usage of life.'

Strausom establishes his own cult, maintaining in a Catholic Church a chapel where a candle is lit for each one of his dead friends—except the one who betrayed him. One day, he meets a lady of his own age, dressed in black, who has been coming regularly to kneel and pray at his 'altar' : she prays—so he learns—for the very friend not honoured by him whom she knew as well and loved. Eventually, Strausom dominates his resentment and adds the missing candle : now his 'altar' is complete, it acquires its real meaning as the sole repository of the memory of dead friends.

The tale is interesting for its denial of death, the desire to examine the relationship between serving memory and the continuation of living, as well as the continual presence of nothingness.

*Is There a Life after Death* (1910) is a curious essay on immortality. It brings out James' deep preoccupation with the 'eternal mystery of things'. His conviction is that '*death . . .*

on the one side . . . means the termination of the consciousness, it means on the other the beginning of the drama in any case in which the consciousness survives. In what case *may* the consciousness be said to survive. . . ?' In pressing this question it is not death or immortality as such that he wishes to discuss for —of their own essence—they seem to be out of reach. They can be reached only through man's projection into them—the very thought that he applies to answer the challenge they pose. Therefore, the problem fascinated James because it is 'a part of our general concern with life', because it is 'a renewal of the interest, the appreciation, the passion, the large and consecrated consciousness, in a word, of which, we have so splendid a sample in this world'. Since the conscience is 'the highest good I can conceive of', 'the fountain of being', 'how can we hold complete disconnection likely?' He cannot believe in a general relapse into nothingness, nor in a transmutation of moral states into a divinely ordered eternity. He believes in a purifying elevation of the terrestrial evolving in the supra-terrestrial, but remaining closely united, pursuing the same quest and experience. He can only consider 'immortality *as* personal, which is the only thing that gives it meaning or relevance . . . , as the accumulation of the very treasure itself of consciousness filling us with the unlimited vision of being'. James would appear to agree with the permanency of the consciousness in the infinity of time-space, which would entail the suppression of the duality of life-death and the existence of a continually changing universal flux—different forms of the same, unique and lasting spiritual essence. (In this, James is close to certain Eastern philosophies.)

F. O. Matthiessen has written of James that 'the projection of the super-conscious was what attached him to the ghost-stories'; the critic Orange that he 'was in love with the next world, or the next state of consciousness; he was always exploring the border land between the conscious and the superconscious. In these extremes, indeed, James seems readily to speculate on the forms of consciousness that extend beyond immediate reality, but he does it more with an artistic approach than philosophical conviction. He is merely experimenting, advancing—with some caution, veiled by vagueness—into this quite uncertain terrain of possibilities and suggestions. He never formulates any religious or metaphysical statements.

Religion is absent from James' works (except for its use as local colour on certain occasions); spiritual life and God have no part in his heroes' tribulations. He remained indifferent to all dogmas and religious beliefs. The Presbyterianism of his family and his father's visionary theories have left almost no trace in his thinking. Nevertheless, he has been considered as 'a purely religious writer', as possessing 'a religious sensibility' on account of his particular, indirect way—through perception and reflection—of seeing life as an infinite process of revelation. In his presentations, he would seem to discuss some finer, mythical undying essence. They are impregnated with and illuminated by a diffused spiritual quality, but one which is not really spiritual. Like those of Proust, his landscapes, characters and material descriptions are endowed with an impalpable and superior significance. Although they recognize no religion and are not spiritually tormented, the principal Jamesian heroes seem to be living according to the tenets of a rigorous faith : their acute sense of conscience, their struggle for good as opposed to evil, their abnegation and their magnanimity are moral qualities akin to those prescribed by the Christian ethics. Their trials and changes always have transcendental overtones; although the notion 'to be saved' (which plays a large part in their preoccupations) has no meaning in regard to eternal salvation in a traditional Christian sense, it presupposes within the individual the most extensive and integral 'salvation' to which the human spirit can attain. Existing in an intensified state of inner and also metaphysical values, they seem only to have been denied Divine Grace.

James offers a poetic and psychological exploration of the supernatural world, since he believes that—as an artist and a novelist—he should not be concerned with ideas and abstractions. 'He had a mind so fine,' writes T. S. Eliot, 'that no idea could violate it.' The existential, metaphysical or spiritual aspects of his work are only latent 'periscopic' formulations : he only approaches from afar 'the chamber of the soul'. This principal interest is man himself, represented as the master of his own life and salvation, aspiring to a moral heroism, an aesthetic idealism and an intensely pure form of humanism. He is not in search of love and peace in God, but of a greater extension of human consciousness. In other words, the Jamesian man can never escape himself nor evade life on this earth.

# *11. The Art of Henry James*

THE LITERARY essays of Henry James, his letters and his *Notebooks* all bear witness to the lucidity and the application, with which he undertook his work as a novelist and critic. 'It is art that makes life,' he wrote 'makes interest, makes importance . . . and I know of no substitute whatever for the force and the beauty of its process.' Little in his existence mattered outside his creative dedication and constant thought about the techniques of writing. He never ceased to elaborate his method and to seek new means of expression. He is one of the most outstanding literary theoreticians of his times, one of those who wished to change the concept and ends of fiction, to turn the genre into an equally aesthetic and psychological medium. He himself succeeded in creating a profoundly original style.

Not an impassive observer, James possesses to an exceptional degree the 'capacity for receiving straight impressions'. He finds his initial ground in an intuitive contact with reality. Considering the novel to be also a form of 'history', he strives for a greater 'density of detail', the typical and striking features that communicate 'the surge and pressure of life'. Few novelists have equalled such examination of the particular world they have chosen to study; few writers have sought so much the descriptive portrayal of reality, to capture its organic unity and truth. Since James distinguishes between 'life being inclusion and confusion, and art being all discrimination and selection', he chooses from among his impressions the one which possesses an exceptional suggestive power, which is best fitted to convey the human 'experience' where it originates. '. . . Most of the stories straining to shape under my hand have sprung from a single small seed. . . . The precious particle—reduced, that is, to its mere fruitful essence. . . . One's subject is in the merest grain, the speck of truth, of beauty, of reality, scarcely visible to the common eye. . . . The artist finds in *his* tiny nugget, washed free of awkward accretions and hammered into a sacred hardness, the very stuff for a clear affirmation, the happiest chance for the indestructible'.

James, however, keeps his inspiration relatively free from submissive reliance upon reality. The latter exists for him beyond its brute matter of evidence and presence. Though he finds in it his 'tiny nugget', each work should be at the same time the 'full demonstration of the fatal futility of Fact' : 'Nine-tenths of the artist's interest with them [the Facts] is that of what he shall add to them and how he shall turn them'. James retains only the moral aspect of his direct outer impressions—the 'idea'. In connexion with a new story, he writes : '*Il faut que ce soit une idée*—it must be an idea—it can't be a "story" in the vulgar sense of the word. It must be a picture; it must illustrate something. God knows that's enough—if the thing *does* illustrate. To make little anecdotes of this kind real *morceaux de vie* is a plan quite inspiring enough. . . . One must put a little action—not a stupid, mechanical arbitrary action, but something that is of the real essence of the subject.' From all the dramatic events that occur to him, James wishes to distil only 'a little organic and effective Action'—only what is *significant*. A reliance on anecdotal material would prevent him from producing the desired effect, would give him 'too little room to turn around'.

To some extent, he wishes to create a kind of vacuum around his 'idea' so that its particular importance can be better perceived : his work has been compared to a closed and empty room—secure from all intrusion—in which chamber music is performed. If he succeeds in a living representation of his subjects within the narrow limits that he imposes upon himself, it is because his method of selection compels him to search out the telling, far reaching, most inclusive detail. In addition, he renders everything more visible by the wake of words, images and suggestions—the very density of association and accumulation—with which he surrounds the central idea, even though this creates some poetic vagueness. He seeks for '. . . foreshortening at any cost, for imparting to patches the value of presences, for dressing objects as in an *air* as of the dimensions they can't possibly have.'

Charles Du Bos writes of James' works that 'finally, the most direct effect is obtained by the most indirect of methods'. The novelist not only chooses rigorously—restrictively, so to say—his bare essential idea, he also wants it to be 'secret and complex', endowed with the greatest 'emotional capacity', bringing out in subtler traits 'only the fine, the large, the human, the natural, the fundamental, the passionate, things'—containing not the mere representation but the concern and 'real solution of the pressing question of life'. He wishes to suggest what remains impalpable and indistinct behind appearances, happenings and man's behaviour. Never openly revealing his 'central idea', he places it in a setting of tension, effects and mystery, relating it to his characters' nature and reactions .

According to André Gide, 'James allows only that amount of steam to escape, which is needed to take his machine forward from one point to another. I cannot think that economy and restraint have ever been used so aptly and yet been taken so far. The proportion between the driving power and the drawing out of the work is always perfect.' The result of this approach is a constant uncertainty, if not a slight obscurity, as the work progresses; the reader feels disturbed about the author's precise intention, ignorant of the operating process which he follows. Avoiding clear, final pronouncements, James wants to be depended upon 'his instinct everywhere—for the *indirect* presentation of his main image'. Indeed, regarding the great masters he admired, he thought that 'one of the most interesting pursuits in the world is to read between the lines of the best literature'. His fiction relies increasingly on the suggestive elements, on personal sensation, on the way in which the author assumes an attitude toward the problem under examination and presents it. 'We talk here, naturally, not of non-poetic forms but of those whose highest bid is addressed to the imagination, to the spiritual and the aesthetic vision, the mind led *captive* by a charm and a spell, and uncalculated art.' In his work, he encompasses his own struggle with reality, seeking to reproduce his 'reflection and perception', 'awareness' and 'individual vision', 'the power to penetrate' with an 'intense consciousness'. He is concerned less with the development of the 'anecdote' and the 'situation' than with the 'sketch, picture, vision'—a 'unity of effect' which will 'illuminate something' as a meaningful image, even though it proceeds from the unidentified source of individual attraction and the drive to creativity. He reveals his materials not as static knowledge, enclosed in limited dimensions, but rather as fluctuating, and unformed, in a flexibility of meanings; it is a question of making 'a presentation, not of sharp particulars, but of loose appearances, vague notions and sounds and symptoms, just perceptible presences and general looming possibilities'. Therefore each work conveys the impression of groping forward rather than advancing, of moving toward a secret explicable only by the course of events, through stages of wonderment and suspicion; there is no straight forward exposition or narrative explosion, only a progress from enigma to revelation, from obscurity to the light. Each work is a patient uncovering of hidden presences, an 'intimate battle with the particular idea, with the subject, the possibility, the place'. James never exaggerates the importance of facts, yet he does not obliterate them with his indirect method : there is a sense of the author's engagement with the material he intends to analyse. His liberties, his complex and almost respectful elaboration, are offered as spontaneous development : he is the one challenged by a given reality, deciphering it in his alert consciousness. Convinced that human actions are not as simple as they seem, that they are difficult to communicate, he is extremely careful to preserve the intrinsic, impenetrable 'innocence' of his material by remaining at a safe distance and approaching it in gradual strokes. He is opposed to overt expression and facility, to 'the terrible fluidity of self-revelation'. He prefers an art which is 'all suggestion and sensation and illumination'.

Once a 'case' has been outlined, James studies it through the consciousness and emotions of his heroes. The particular conflict arises from their intense confrontation with reality, from the vibrations and repercussions that it provokes in their sensitive, speculative minds: 'There are', James writes, 'few things more exciting to me, in short, than a psychological reason.' Moreover he situates his probing behind the external, evident manifestation of feelings and behaviour; he tries to elucidate the difficulties implied in the essence of his subject, in the complexity of his heroes' tormented psyche and the efforts required by the elaborate solution. This examination is an attempt to reach the 'deeper psychology'. The dramatic development of the plot is resolved through the mental affinities of the heroes, through their sensations mysteriously communicated or exchanged, and the mutual analysis in which they persist: 'It is in the chemistry of these subtle substances, these curious precipitates and explosive gases which are suddenly formed by the contact of mind with mind,' writes T. S. Eliot, 'that James is unequalled.' The progression of a book consists in the heroes' progressive states of consciousness, with all its smallest fluctuations and drawbacks. The reader—in turn—as the author and the protagonist, follows the same uneasy path of patient exploration and wondering, even to the extent that he gradually feels transported from the actions and the reality which James wishes to apprehend. The heroes, reduced to their interior mechanisms, occasionally become less vivid, less believable. James was aware of the dangers of such treatment; sometimes he knew that a specific subject could be 'too inclusively psychological . . . that it depends too little on incident'.

'Semi-conscious' states alternate with the more intense states of consciousness : the heroes—in their common confrontation— seem to exist with the purpose of knowing each other and acquiring an ever 'expending consciousness' of life. 'Finely aware', 'deep', 'immense', they cannot emerge from their inwardness, compelled endlessly to analyse feelings and attitudes, motives and intentions, without admitting simple explanations or resorting to decisive solutions. Attracted by unfathomable presences within and around themselves, there are 'things they had a manifest consciousness of not saying' : 'It was the unsaid that occupied them—the thing they had been going round and round without naming it.' Also, as in Maggie Verver's case, 'the specific, in almost any direction was utterly forbidden her. . . . She was learning, almost from minute to minute, to be a mistress of shades.'

On the other hand, the heroes being 'face to face with a crisis of . . . destiny', must travel a route that requires constant and considerable vigilance; they need to evaluate and reassess their least action for its immediate results or far-reaching consequences. Although their final experiences might be a 'great negative adventure', the effect of the world on them and on their interior evolution is not lost. They are motivated by emotions and considerations common to all humanity, yet they seem mysterious and exceptional because they live with intensity in their minds and allow an excessive importance to what happens to them. 'We have tremendous perceptions', they declare. 'What is splendid . . . is the extraordinary freedom . . . of our intercourse and the fact that we do care—so independently of our personal interests, with so little selfishness or other vulgarity.' Their restraint, their fear of committing themselves to communication determines the increasing rôle played by the stream of consciousness; in James' works this is not subconscious flow of dreamlike associations, but an interior monologue or deliberation. Life seems real, permanent only to the extent that it has been felt through a 'mute agitation', 'a long term of conscious contact'—and is enriched by many uncertainties and possibilities.

There is a certain gratuitousness in the closed universe of James' fiction. The characters themselves appear to be imprisoned; never free from the presence of others, nor from their tumultuous consciousness, their nature and situations are magnified to exceptional, artificial proportions. Their problems are sometimes simple, but the solutions are far from being so;

the decisive, analytical approach, the perptual wondering and hesitancy accumulate evidence far beyond what the case entails. It is submerged with its original objectives by the process of handling and exploration. The subtle incursions and connotations finally provoke a general blurring—an opposite effect from the clarification sought at the beginning. This apparently gratuitous method which leads the reader 'astray', if not exactly nowhere, is none the less justifiable as poetry and suggestive symbolism : it enables the work of art to pass beyond the limits imposed by structure and time, giving it an allegorical and—almost—universal character.

Intellect would appear to be the motivation for James' works, in the infallibly logical selection of detail and overall plan, in the power to search the most obscure recesses of the soul. The characters themselves possess unusual powers of judgement and discrimination. But ultimately intuition, rather than intellect—controlling James' initial inspiration, accounting for the collection and re-evaluation of perceptions—would appear to advance the story. It is also one of the heroes' major qualities, and above all the heroines', as women are more often the protagonists in James' works. The primary reliance on intuition makes his works difficult to read, for this process—more subject to ramification and unexpected allusions—creates a constant tension, a cumulative drawing out of the style. The instances of conscious thinking intervene to restore the equilibrium, re-stating perceptions in the reality of the mind. In other words, intellect and intuition react upon each other in a close and continuous relationship.

To allow his 'gradual revelation' to achieve 'a certain illusion', 'the image of life', James adopts techniques of presentaion which correspond to his psychological approach through subject-matter. His 'economy' of art presupposes 'point of view', 'reflectors', 'centres', 'lights'. The point of view—the 'central intelligence'—is the particular angle chosen from which to examine a situation and tell a story : it is a witness observing and recording or a protagonist's consciousness. The method is more original when the hero, no longer enjoying the function of simple narrator, becomes the prism through which the plot and the other characters are refracted. Nothing is illuminated by the same, uniform light; nothing happens outside the individual's capacity to observe or participate, which can relate but certain things—only what it sees and knows. For example, in *The Turn of the Screw*, the reader is introduced to the mind of the governess—where all the real and imagined events occur; in *The Ambassadors,* Strether is present in all the scenes, related as he sees them, even though he is not the narrator and is not directly aware of his consciousness; in *The Golden Bowl,* the plot is centred successively upon the personalities of the prince and the princess. Whatever the 'point of view' adopted, James identifies himself with his particular protagonist, who becomes his 'point of view' and, so to say, is writing the story for him. He is not the 'omniscient author' who pretends to tell and explain everything in an even effort of interest and understanding. The writing of the story is simultaneous with the experience of the hero as it is being lived. There is no separation between the occurrence and the revelation of action or its significance. Moreover, the hero narrating or the hero's consciousness, in expanding or distorting the reality, offer finally a more flexible, plausible play of effects and contrasts: the representation is personal, unilateral, uneven, and so far more appealing and true; with its inadequacy or incompleteness, it seems as if seized upon living matter. For James, 'there is no economy of treatment without an adopted, a related point of view'.

He extends this method. All the characters of a novel become 'reflectors', to a degree, mutually revealing various aspects of themselves by virtue of the 'lights' they throw upon one another's analyses. This is part of the Jamesian 'scenic presentation' or 'picture', strongly marked in his development after 1890 and his attempt to write for the stage. For example, such novels as *The Awkward Age,* might almost be plays and can be sub-divided into acts and scenes: dialogue is almost continuous throughout, whereas descriptions and actions are reduced to a minimum. The novels turn upon certain 'centres of consciousness', progress from one 'centre of revelation' to another, focusing upon only two or three characters and a small number of significant confrontations. In this way the representation of life is far more dramatic and vivid.

The settings are generally subordinated to the main psychological concern. Although extremely characteristic in themselves, they are not allowed to interfere with the action, being only gradually introduced by means of the protagonists' perceptions and associations. Seen thus through successive states of mind, they acquire a revelatory function and contribute to the psychological probing as well, while assuming an overall moral and symbolic presence more or less detached from other material appearance. Strether's walks *(The Ambassadors)* in the Luxembourg gardens or in the country are examples of this impressionistic refracted method, which links the environment to mental reactions and feelings. In *The Wings of the Dove,* Densher's first impressions of Mrs Lowder's drawing-room illuminate her character and seem to outline his future attitude toward her : '. . . As he walked to and fro, however, taking in the message of her massive florid furniture, the immense expression of her signs and symbols, he had a little doubt of the inconvenience he was prepared to suffer . . . as almost abnormally affirmative, so aggressively erect, were the huge, heavy objects that syllabled his hostess' story. . . . He handn't known . . . that he should "mind" so much how an independent lady might decorate her house. It was the language of the house itself that spoke to him, writing out for him, with surpassing breadth and freedom, the associations and conceptions, the ideals and possibilities of the mistress.'

James' dialogues are extremely subtle, constructed in conformity with his precise governance of effects. The insistence upon certain words, the misapprehensions and intentional vagueness of others, produce particular expressive suggestions beyond actual meaning. The selection, placing and rapport of rejoinders are so minutely planned that one can speak of the mechanics or the artificiality of Jamesian dialogue, which has been termed a 'cerebral version of Marivaux'. Even the pauses and silences have rules, for the meaningful nuance is often to be found in what the characters say imperfectly or deliberately do *not* say. Part of James' power is that he can make us feel that this is so. Characters may talk of harmless and trivial subjects in a pleasant setting, but the unusual associations and omissions which accompany their conversations reveal them at the same time as tormented by fear, apprehension or despair. James' power is to introduce the reader to these oblique, abrupt, shimmering innuendoes, while erasing at every step the traces of details and creating a moral atmosphere of allusions.

James achieves his difficult effects also through exceptional language and style. His early works, which rely on plot development, are written in a more conventionally precise narrative prose. In the second half of his career he adopts a more elaborate, individual means of expression. He is increasingly convinced that 'form *alone* takes and holds and preserves' and that the novelist's rôle is not only to provide an overall structural unity but also to 'charge language with the maximum degree of meaning'.

The Jamesian sentence is marked by the psychological tension which it attempts to express, even when it preserves the aspect of conversational spontaneity or informal construction of thought. Often difficult and complex, it follows a secret order and rhythm, patiently evolves around strategic words conveying the impression of a thought in the process of structuring and defining. It gropes always for finer precisions until it reaches a determining statement. A good example is the sentence in *The Wings of the Dove* which portrays Densher's attitude to Kate's aunt, Mrs Lowder : 'This awkwardness of his conscience, both in respect to his general plasticity, the fruit of his feeling plasticity within limits, to be a mode of life like another—certainly better than some, and particularly in respect of such confusion as might reign about what he had really come for—this inward ache was not wholly dispelled by the style, charming as that was, of Kate's poetic versions'. Or there is the description of a meeting between Densher and

Milly: 'She was never—did he understand?—to be one of the afflicted for him; and in the manner in which he understood it something of the answering pleasure that he couldn't help knowing he showed, constituted, he was very soon after to acknowledge, something like a start for intimacy'.

James enriches his vocabulary with abstractions and moral terminology; he endows certain words with new emotional implications by their position or context. In such instances he attains the ultimate in his preference for intuitive 'associations', for the 'fine silver thread of association', which leads through the meander of unidentified shadows, half-lit images and deep perceptions. His style is rarely flamboyant or aggressive, and only succeeds in its effect by means of its multiple suggestions. In the last novel James' prose moves nearer to poetry, to symbolism, and more stress is placed on metaphors. These are mostly visual, arising from an intimate connexion between impressions and feelings, between objects and mental reactions: they eventually coalesce to produce a single conscious knowledge or inner vision. In *The Golden Bowl*, to show Maggie's consciousness of 'recent change in her life', James selects the following image: 'This situation has been occupying, for months and months, the very centre of the garden of her life, but it had reared itself there like some strange, tall tower of ivory, or perhaps rather some wonderful, beautiful, but outlandish pagoda, a structure plated with hard, bright porcelain, coloured and figured and adorned, at the overhanging eaves with silver bells that tinkled, ever so charmingly, when stirred by chance airs. She had walked round and round it—that was what she felt; she had carried on her existence in the space left her for circulation, a space that sometimes seemed ample and sometimes narrow: looking up, all the while at the fair structure that spread itself so amply and rose so high, but never quite making out, as yet, where she might have entered had she wished.'

This metaphor is sustained throughout yet another page, for most of James' metaphors are not intended to have a momentary effect; schematically and deliberately functioning as a *leitmotiv*, their meaning is gradually developed, and becomes explicit and exhausted only at the end of work. The novels *The Wings of the Dove*, *The Golden Bowl*, *The Sacred Fount*, the stories *The Figure in the Carpet* and *The Beast in the Jungle* develop images already suggested in their titles. This symbolistic tendency is more apparent in the last works, where strange, coincidental presences and signs—to various degrees, favourable or menacing—accompany and influence the fictional events. In this way, the hero is oppressed not only by the sight of his situations or interior life; he finds himself surrounded by the hidden, dense universe of portents, symbolic connexions and forebodings.

James passed through several stages in his development, constantly renewing and improving his technique. He attempted various types of narrative fiction : realism, satire, lyricism, symbolism and psychological analysis; he was always eager to discover a highly personal style, the ideal structure and approach which could best provide an illusion of life. Though preoccupied with problems of composition and style, he cannot be classed among the practitioners of 'art for art's sake' or the Victorian aesthetes. His organic method is based on an intimate relationship with the moral life of his characters, expressing simultaneously the two poles of their universe—'experience' and 'consciousness'. It strives to reproduce the groping, perceptive process of the 'self' exposed to the world—selecting, eliminating, refracting, illuminating—in order to reach a deeper reality behind appearances. James believed that 'the whole of anything is never told; you can take only what groups together'. Hence his concern is to portray connexions, reciprocal exchanges rather than restricted inert, constituent elements. He follows the pattern of a gradual revelation. The 'power to guess the unseen from the seen', James said of literary creation, 'to trace the implication of things, to judge the whole piece by the pattern, the condition of feeling life in general so completely that you are well on your way to knowing any particular corner of it—this cluster of gifts may almost be said to constitute experience . . .' for the artist.

James' desire to create a 'picture', a 'vision', approximates more to the intention of a painter or a poet than to that of a novelist. He needs a strong 'principle of cohesion', an 'organic form', to unify his scattered, richly endowed impressions and obtain 'something admirably compact and select', the 'rare compression' that projects and signifies. The rough outer materials of life are only functional to his 'economy' whose effects must be both 'deep-breathing' and 'most magnificent masterly vivid'. The notion of beauty—of art—appears in his work as the only absolute, as a special sphere of permanence. His increasingly complex symbolism and evocative style are used not so much to make his fiction interesting and perceptive as to produce a reshuffling of current and known values. He strives, as it were, to effect a transubstantiation or reality—into the quality of art, into the feeling of having touched on the unknown, the permanently real, perfection. James found fulfilment in this quest for a complete form of expression: his aesthetic ideal implies an affirmative gesture of hope, a kind of salvation in 'the luminous paradise of art'.

# 12. Henry James Today

THE TWENTIETH CENTURY has emerged as the age of the American novel. Never, since Cooper, Poe and Whitman, have American writers been held in more esteem: Dos Passos, Steinbeck, Hemingway and Faulkner, to name only a few, have won international recognition. The great precursor of this trend was Henry James—through the originality of his genius and the quality of his writing. Relatively ignored during his lifetime, and almost forgotten after his death, he was 'discovered' by critics and readers some twenty years ago: he is now considered to be one of the most significant modern novelists. Numerous articles and full-length studies are devoted to him; his works are widely translated and re-edited; they have been adapted for stage, screen and opera.

James wrote between 1864 and 1915, passing through the stages of romanticism, realism and naturalism, before coming to the modern psychological novel. The literary tendencies of an entire epoch or, rather, of several epochs in America, England and France, would seem to be represented in his works. As it develops, his writing foretells the end of a certain way of life and of certain aesthetic ideals in a transitional period when 19th-century methods were rapidly becoming outdated. Like Dostoevski, the explorer of yet unknown fields in literature, he contributed to the re-orientation of the novel, more so than other contemporary writers. He appears closer to contemporary literature than W. D. Howells or Mark Twain in America, Meredith or Hardy in England. He has been called an American Proust; like Proust, he created his personal, analytical way of seeing and describing: he found new means of expression for the material of fiction. His novels are praised today as 'classics'. As a voluntary exile from America, a foreigner in Europe and detached from everyday realities of both continents, he was the first truly international writer; he died forty years ago, wrote at a period relatively distant from our own, however, without really belonging to it : he cannot be associated with a localized past or present, but rather a universal literature.

His work is devoid of conventional descriptive and narrative elements; it not only witnesses but criticizes the manners and life of an age. It depicts an intense conflict with evil in an increasingly absurd world. It is also imbued with a subjective tension, arising from the author's essential solitude, from his desire for fuller participation in existence and his continuous battle with the exigencies of his art. It is an all-out attempt to gratify a deep need for affirmation through the liberating process of creativity. Above all, James can be counted among the initiators of modern psychological realism who have sought for the hidden essence of man and his tragic condition in the world. His analytical method is so penetrating that it endows his books with an aesthetic harmony, a moral significance, an ethics of experience—all sustained by a most acute contact with others and sensibility to life. He is an apostle of the individual's liberty and ideals, condemning restrictive conventions and material interests. His characters—in their conflict with evil, refusal of happiness and acceptance of fate—live on a heroic level of self-realization, possessing a fuller responsibility and consciousness, although at times their moral grandeur would seem to spring from their unfitness to face real commitments. They follow an existential development, free from the intervention of divine or deterministic law. Their heroism consists precisely in a desire to participate with an ever-perceptive intensity in an existence to which they no longer submit, but which they create and dominate according to their intrinsic needs and higher ambitions. The central theme—'the figure in the carpet'—of James' works would appear to be this striving to identify experience with the greatest possible deployment of human sensibility and conscience.

James is also recognized as a novelist in advance of his own times for his artistic method and his style—forerunners of the stream of consciousness and modern symbolism. Inspired by the nineteenth-century novelists, such as Flaubert or George Eliot, he attributed an ever exacting importance to structure and development of narrative evolvement, impressionistic presentation and dramatic dialogue. He was to influence a generation of new writers: in criticism, Ezra Pound and T. S. Eliot; in fiction, Joseph Conrad, Katherine Mansfield and Virginia Woolf in England; Edith Wharton, Scott Fitzgerald and Ernest Hemingway in America. His work can be said above all, to point to the achievements of James Joyce, Proust, Faulkner; and more than those of the 20's and the 30's, the writers of the post-war period feel an affinity with him.

James did not belong to a particular school or group: he occupies a unique position in literature—like Proust, Joyce or D. H. Lawrence. This is not so much because of his inventive genius as a special mode of relationship to the world, to himself and creation—an extremely flexible, sensitive relationship, always halfway between reserve and intensity, suggestion and silence. His work appears as a kind of mysterious ritual to be approached in a state of humble exaltation; the patient, subtle and sometimes obscure accumulation of effects leads to a certain clarity and unity, but still leaves a sense of something beyond the apparent statements and vision.

In his groping pursuit always to discover deeper revelations—psychological and, almost, metaphysical—James does not only wish to portray man's relation to society and destiny: he also proposes a set of guiding principles, an ethics for the individual's rôle in existence that turns upon abnegation and sublimation of the self. Disconnected from reality, conscious of a lack, the Jamesian hero converts his unconditional liberty into personal assuagement—the sense of having lived—not happiness; overcoming his inadequacy and external limitations, he must carry out a kind of miraculous *tour de force*: a transfiguration of the impossibility to live fully into the possibility of fully attaining the moral potentiality to live. Technically, the stories seem to follow the same pattern of uneasy struggle and reversal : escaping their own logic, leading to the least expected solutions, reverting to their initial point. On both levels, psychological and aesthetic, one finds the constant interplay of opposites, an indivisible duality between failure and success, advancement and retreat, clarification and bewilderment, concentration and dispersion. . . . In the very progression of his works, James never fails to include a sense of crumbling reality and incapacity of being. A sort of osmosis is ultimately reached : both separation and belonging, a desired fusion and an inevitable isolation of man and of art in relation to the world and the unknown possibilities of the human consciousness. At this crossroads of nowhere, of multivalences and contrasts, James mysteriously approaches other, far-extending latitudes—as if this Jamesland, always deeply penetrated, remains none the less always insufficiently explored and is to be revisited.

James' work occupies more than fifty volumes; although sometimes it may appear cold and abstract, it displays an essential richness and mastery. 'There you have', wrote William Dean Howells, 'the work of a great psychologist, who has the imagination of a poet, the wit of a keen humorist, the conscience of an impeccable moralist, the temperament of a philosopher, and the wisdom of a rarely experienced witness of the world. . . .'

*An Unpublished Letter From Henry James to Minnie and Paul Bourget*[1]

February 23rd 1888
De Vere Gardens

My dear Friend,

I would have replied before now to your eloquent and subtle letter from Milan, had I felt equal to entering into a debate with you on the important questions that you raise. The blame can also be laid on the life I lead here : I scribble away all the morning, but at the same time I am almost entirely prevented from indulging in any disinterested correspondence. Had I not been prevented from doing so, I should already have have informed you how admirable and eminently acceptable I find your sensitive reaction to the remarks and reservations I allowed myself to make in relation to *Mensonges*. The way in which you welcome my severity does you the greatest credit and makes me almost blush. It has the effect of making me regret all the more surely that an intellect like your own should have thought it necessary to make so great a sacrifice to false gods! For I still find them false, my dear friend, despite your arguments and despite your magnanimity—I find the point of view, tone, matter and style of *Mensonges* vain and mistaken.

[1] This letter (a translation from James' French original) allows the reader only a very small insight into James' way of life, concerns and friendships. It was written to his most intimate French friends; nevertheless, it differs somewhat in tone from the letters he wrote to closer friends, in England and in America. It is included here as throwing some light on a rather neglected aspect of James' life.

To my mind, your characters are so lacking in *importance*, that I remain quite astonished when I find you expending so extreme a care upon their peculiarities. Above all, this is true of Mme Moraines, whom you exaggerate (and upon whose minor physical behaviour and minute details of toilet you lavish too great an attention) in the most unwonted manner, as an *illustration* (in the English sense) of life. But I am truly mystified when I find you going over to her side, so to speak (without seeming aware of this) and when you relate events from her point of view, speaking as if through *her* mind, giving a detailed account of her arguments, *her* fears, anguish and hopes. We do not want it and we do not believe in it! A subjective Mme Moraines is an unpleasant joke; she is subjective only because you want her to be so, and—unfortunately—you want this because, despite the infinite variety of life, you devote to her and to her *underclothing* a quite particular and unwholesome attention—not to speak of a gift for interpretation, a sympathetic power of imagination, worthy, as one would say, of a better cause. What moral 'centre' could there be to a creature like that! I am sorry to think that you should strive to provide her with one—as if that were all that life contained. But such a nature is so great an impoverishment of life as it really is, that the reader is insulted and imposed upon when you invite him to take up this work under the pretext of giving him a psychology of suffering! My dear friend, you must listen to me and give it all up: it is far too grubby a business. As for your young writers, to me they seem no more substantial. There is the fellow who lashes out in anger at his mistress, and who succumbs to an almost mortal sickness because he had thought her to be an angel of purity—a woman about whom all he knew was that she was in the habit of being unfaithful to her husband with every indication of ease, and that she was coming to sleep with him in broad daylight in the room next to his sister's, before he had even asked her to do so! Perhaps I am not entirely aware of your intentions with regard to Vincy, for I must inform you—and you must have realized, too—that we have a strong aversion to this character who so often appears in French novels: the sensitive and eminent young man beginning his first adulterous affair. Almost our only reaction to him—as Anglo-Saxons—is a desire to give him a good kick in the behind. He is above all distasteful when he is a poet or when he is presented to us as a superior soul; I assure you that his presence quite marred my enjoyment of your other characters.

You tell me that Paris is full of Suzannes, of Desforges, of Renés and of Vincys; this is equivalent to saying that life is full of wretchedness and dirt. But that is no reason for cramming our heads with it. The greater the range of other things in life, the less room there is for these creatures. You will tell me again that to talk of 'dirt' is to beg the question, and that it is an essential characteristic of life. If love is primarily to be distinguished thus, yes; but I think one is taking too much upon oneself if one affirms this without knowing the truth of each individual case, and above all if one depicts this subject only in its minor aspects (by 'minor aspects' I mean precise details that concern only those who practise them, such as the number of embraces, their quality, the place where the encounter takes place, the way in which it is done, and a thousand other intensely personal details which are less capable of open delineation than anything else in the world). What can one know of these matters as far as they concern others and how can one speak about all this on behalf of anyone other than oneself? For this reason it is preferable to talk of them as little as possible, for if one speaks of them as they concern oneself, the result is fatuous, tasteless and immodest. For me, the conduct of love seems to constitute a very special part of our existence, essentially characterized by *action* and not by thought. This element of action is the affair of each one of us, but as soon as thought is brought to bear upon it—as soon as one drabbles intellectually in the matter, as a novelist or as a painter, it becomes unhealthy and distasteful. And that is why infinite tact and taste are required unless one should flounder in the mud: it is a question of treatment, an entirely practical problem. You should not be shocked when I tell you that in your case every page seems to me to lack precisely this tact and this taste! How can these things possibly concern us—the details of Desforges' flirtations or of the love-making of René and his mistress and the state of disarray of the shirts or corsets worn? I should never wish to know what happens between a man and a woman in their bedroom and in their bed; and I really cannot see what difference (above all with regard to publicity) is made to the matter by the fact that these persons are not married.

I know that you are now in Paris, having been told by a good lady with whom I am acquainted here that her brother-in-law, Lord Lytton, had spoken with you and that he found the meeting most agreeable. I hope that the distractions of life in the capital will enable you to sustain the almost feminine length at which I have written. I occasionally see Jusserand here and find him particularly likeable. He has given me reasons to look forward to your book on Balzac—in which I hope to find the real Bourget again. Urbin Mengin writes me some pleasing and almost plaintive letters (how engagingly he writes!), from which I deduce that he does not shape well at English. I think he reads too much of your work—and that is no way to learn the language of your harsh though faithful friend, Henry James.

## I—WORKS BY JAMES

A. NOVELS AND SHORT STORIES (The date given is that of first book publication; if American, it is given in brackets.)

*A Passionate Pilgrim and Other Tales,* 1875.

*Roderick Hudson,* 1876.

*The American,* 1877.

*Watch and Ward,* 1878.

*The Europeans,* 1878.

*Daisy Miller,* 1878.

*An International Episode,* 1878.

*The Madonna of the Future; Longstaff's Marriage; Madame de Mauves; Eugene Pickering; The Diary of a Man of Fifty; Benvolio,* 1879. *Confidence,* 1879.

*Washington Square; The Pension Beaurepas; A Bundle of Letters,* 1880. *The Portrait of a Lady,* 1881.

*The Siege of London; The Point of View,* 1883.

*Tales of Three Cities; The Impressions of a Cousin; Lady Barbarina; A New England Winter,* 1884.

*Stories Revived*: I. *The Author of Beltraffio; Pandora; The Path of Duty; A Day of Days; A Light Man*; II. *Georgina's Reasons; A Passionate Pilgrim; A Landscape Painter; Rose-Agathe*; III. *Poor Richard; The Last of Valerii; Master Eustace; The Romance of Certain Old Clothes; A Most Extraordinary Case,* 1885.

*The Bostonians,* 1886.

*The Princess Casamassima*, 1886.

*The Reverberator*, 1888.

*The Aspern Papers*; *Louisa Pallant*; *The Modern Warning*, 1888.

*A London Life*; *The Patagonia*; *The Liar*; *Mrs Temperley*, 1889.

*The Tragic Muse*, 1890.

*The Lesson of the Master*; *The Marriages*; *The Pupil*; *Brooksmith*; *The Solution*; *Sir Edmund Orme*, 1892.

*The Real Thing*, 1893.

*The Private Life*; *The Wheel of Time*; *Lord Beaupré*; *The Visits*; *Collaboration*; *Owen Wingrave*, 1893.

*Terminations*; *The Death of the Lion*; *The Coxon Fund; The Middle Years*; *The Altar of the Dead*, 1895.

*Embarrassments*; *The Figure in the Carpet*; *Glasses*; *The Next Time*; *The Way it Came*, 1896.

*The Other House*, 1896.

*The Spoils of Poynton*, 1897.

*What Maisie Knew*, 1897.

*In The Cage*, 1898.

*The Two Magics*; *The Turn of the Screw*; *Covering End*, 1898.

*The Awkward Age*, 1899.

*The Soft Side; The Great Good Place; 'Europe'; Paste; The Real Right Thing*; *The Great Condition*; *The Tree of Knowledge*; *The Abasement of the Northmores*; *The Given Case*; *John Delavoy*; *The Third Person*; *Maud-Evelyn*; *Miss Gunton of Poughkeepsie*, 1900.

*The Sacred Fount*, 1901.

*The Wings of the Dove*, 1902.

*The Better Sort*; *Broken Wings*; *The Beldonald Holbein*; *The Two Faces*; *The Tone of Time*; *The Special Type*; *Mrs Medwin*; *Flickerbridge*; *The Story in It*; *The Beast in the Jungle*; *The Birthplace*; *The Papers*, 1903.

*The Ambassadors*, 1903.

*The Golden Bowl*, 1904.

*Fordham Castle*; *The Jolly Corner*; *Julia Bride*, 1909.

*The Finer Grain*; *The Velvet Glove*; *Mora Montravers*; *A Round of Visits*; *Crapy Cornelia*; *The Bench of Desolation*, 1910.
*The Outcry*, 1911.
*The Ivory Tower*, 1917.
*The Sense of the Past*, 1917.


Collected Editions :

*The Novels and Tales of Henry James*, 26 volumes, Scribner (New York) 1907-1917.
*The Novels and Stories of Henry James*, 35 volumes, Macmillan (London) 1921-23.

Many of the novels and short stories are now available in inexpensive paperback editions published by The New American Library (New York) in the Signet Classics series, and by Penguin Books (Harmondsworth, England).

B. PLAYS

*The Complete Plays of Henry James*, edited by Leon Edel, New York and London, 1949.

C. CRITICISM

*French Poets and Novelists*, London and New York, 1878 and 1893.

*Hawthorne*, London, 1879.

*Partial Portraits*, London, 1888, 1894 and 1899.

*Essays in London and Elsewhere*, London and New York, 1893.

*The Art of the Novel* (Critical prefaces by James), ed. R.P. Blackmur, New York, 1934; London, 1935.

*The Scenic Art* : *Notes on Acting and the Drama, 1872-1901*, ed. Allan Wade, New Brunswick, N.J., 1948; London, 1949.

*The Art of Fiction and Other Essays*, ed. Morris Roberts, New York, 1948.

*The American Essays*, ed. Leon Edel, New York, 1956.

*The Painter's Eye* : *Notes and Essays on the Pictorial Arts*, ed.
    J. L. Sweeney, Cambridge, Mass., 1956; London, 1956.
*The House of Fiction*, ed. Leon Edel, London, 1957.
*Literary Reviews and Essays on American, English and French
    Literature*, ed. Albert Mordell, New York, 1957.

D.  TRAVEL

*Portraits of Places*, Boston, 1883; London, 1883 (New York,
    1948).
*A Little Tour in France*, Boston, 1884.
*English Hours*, New York and London, 1905.
*The American Scene*, New York and London, 1907 (with an
    introduction by W. H. Auden, New York, 1946).
*Italian Hours*, London, 1909.

E.  BIOGRAPHY

*William Wetmore Story and his Friends*, London and New
    York, 1903 (London, 1957).

G.  AUTOBIOGRAPHICAL WRITINGS AND LETTERS

*Henry James* : *Autobiography*, ed. F. W. Dupee, New York
    and London, 1956.
This edition contains the following :
*A Small Boy and Others* (New York and London, 1913);
    *Notes of a Son and Brother* (New York and London,
    1914); *The Middle Years* (New York and London, 1917).
*The Letters of Henry James*, ed. Percy Lubbock, 2 vols., New
    York and London, 1920.
*Henry James and Robert Louis Stevenson: A Record of Friend-
    ship and Criticism*, ed. Janet Adam Smith, London, 1948.
*The Selected Letters of Henry James*, ed. Leon Edel, New
    York, 1955; London, 1956.
*Henry James and H. G. Wells* : *A Record of their Friendship,
    their Debate on the Art of Fiction, and the Quarrel*, ed.
    Leon Edel and Gordon N. Ray, London, 1958.
*The Notebooks of Henry James*, ed. F. O. Matthiessen and
    Kenneth B. Murdock, New York and London, 1947.

## II.—Works on James

ANDERSON, Quentin: *The American Henry James,* New Brunswick, N. J., 1957; London, 1958.

BEACH, J. W.: *The Method of Henry James*, New Haven, Conn., 1918; London, 1918.

BEWLEY, *Marius*: *The Complex Fate*, London, 1952; New York, 1954. *The Eccentric Design: Form in the Classic American Novel*, London, 1959; New York, 1959.

BLACKMUR, R. P.: 'Henry James', in *Literary History of the United States*, ed. R. E. Spiller et al., Vol. 2, New York, 1948.

BROOKS, Van Wyck: *The Pilgrimage of Henry James*, New York, 1955.

CLAIR, John A., *The Ironic Dimension in the Fiction of Henry James*, Pittsburgh, Penn., 1966.

DUPEE, F. W. (ed.) *The Question of Henry James: A Collection of Critical Essays*, New York, 1945; London, 1947.

DUPEE, F. W.: *Henry James*, New York and London, 1951.

EDEL, Leon: *The Life of Henry James*: I. *The Untried Years;* II. *The Conquest of London*; III. *The Middle Years,* Philadelphia and London, 1953-1963.

EDGAR, Pelham: *Henry James, Man and Author*, London, 1925.

GREENE, Graham: 'Henry James: the religious aspect', in *Contemporary Essays*, London, 1933.

GREENE, Graham: 'Henry James: the Private universe', in *The English Novelists*, London, 1936.

KETTLE, Arnold: 'Henry James: *The Portrait of a Lady*', in *An Introduction to the English Novel*, Vol. 2, London, 1953.

LEAVIS, F. R.: 'Henry James' in *The Great Tradition*, London and New York, 1948.

MATTHIESSEN, F. O.: *Henry James, The Major Phase*, London and New York, 1944. *The James Family: An Anthology*, New York, 1947.

NOWELL-SMITH, S. (ed.): *The Legend of the Master*, London, 1947; New York, 1948.

POIRIER, William R.: *The Comic Sense of Henry James*, New York and London, 1960.

POUND, Ezra: 'Henry James', in *Literary Essays of Henry James*, ed. T. S. Eliot, London, 1954.

TRILLING, Lionel: 'The Princess Casamassima', in *The Liberal Imagination*, New York, 1950; London, 1951.

TRILLING, Lionel: 'The Bostonians', in *The Opposing Self*, New York and London, 1955.

WILSON, Edmund: 'The Ambiguity of Henry James', in *The Triple Thinkers*, London, 1952.

WINTERS, Yvor: 'Maule's Well, or Henry James and the Relation of Morals to Manners', in *In Defence of Reason*, New York, 1947.

ZABEL, Morton Dauwen: *Craft and Character in Modern Fiction*, New York and London, 1957.

This selected bibliography is, of course, not exhaustive. The reader is advised to consult *A Bibliography of Henry James* by Leon Edel and Dan H. Laurence (London, 1957) which supersedes the earlier *A Bibliography of the Writings of Henry James,* by Le Roy Phillips (1930).

1843          (15th April). Born in New York.

1855–1860  Travels in Europe.

1861–1863  Resides at Newport and Cambridge, Mass.

1864–1869  Début as a writer.

1870–1874  Further travels in Europe.

1875–1876  Makes a definitive move to Europe : to Paris first, and then London.

1874–1881  The international theme : *Roderick Hudson* (1875), *The American* (1877), *Daisy Miller* (1878), *The Portrait of a Lady* (1881).

1885–1890  The social novel : *The Bostonians* (1885), *The Princess Casamassima* (1886), *The Tragic Muse* (1890).

1890–1895  Writes for the stage; his plays are unsuccessful : *Guy Domville* (1895).

1895–1915  The major stage of his career; short stories : *The Death of the Lion* (1894), *The Figure in the Carpet* (1896). *The Turn of the Screw* (1898), *The Jolly Corner* (1909). Novels : *The Spoils of Poynton* (1897), *The Awkward Age* (1898), *The Wings of the Dove* (1902), *The Ambassadors* (1903), *The Golden Bowl* (1904).

1916          (28th February). Dies in London.